国家林业和草原局普通高等教育"十四五"规划教材

中华农耕文明
（下册）

胡家英　主编

中国林业出版社

图书在版编目（CIP）数据

中华农耕文明. 下 / 胡家英主编. —北京：中国林业出版社，2022.7（2024.5重印）
国家林业和草原局普通高等教育"十四五"规划教材
ISBN 978-7-5219-1697-3

Ⅰ.①中… Ⅱ.①胡… Ⅲ.①农业—英语—高等学校—教材 Ⅳ.①S

中国版本图书馆CIP数据核字（2022）第085843号

中国林业出版社·教育分社

策划、责任编辑：曹鑫茹　　责任校对：苏　梅
电话：（010）83143560　　传真：（010）83143516

出版发行	中国林业出版社（100009　北京市西城区刘海胡同7号）
	E-mail: jiaocaipublic@163.com　电话：（010）83143500
	http://www.forestry.gov.cn/lycb.html
印　刷	北京中科印刷有限公司
版　次	2022年7月第1版
印　次	2024年5月第2次印刷
开　本	787mm×1092mm　1/16
印　张	9.5
字　数	270千字
定　价	36.00元

未经许可，不得以任何方式复制或抄袭本书之部分或全部内容。
版权所有　侵权必究

《中华农耕文明》（下册）编写人员

主　编　胡家英

副主编　宋宝梅

编　者　满　盈　潘秋阳　岳　欣　殷际文

序
Foreword

  东北农业大学胡家英教授多年从事农业院校本科、硕士、博士英语教学，对涉农语言文化进行深入研究，为宣传中国传统农耕文化，编写了《中华农耕文明》（上、下册）。2021 年 8 月教育部印发的《加强和改进涉农高校耕读教育工作方案》明确提出要加强学生传统农业文化教育，将耕读教育相关课程作为涉农专业学生必修课。《中华农耕文明》（上、下册）的出版，对弘扬我国耕读优秀传统文化，加强大学生传统农业文化教育，促进农业特色通识教育，培养"大国三农"情怀将起到积极作用。

  《中华农耕文明》（上、下册）的编写坚持语言、文化、思维能力同步提高的教学理念，坚持课程思政，弘扬中国优秀传统文化，增强民族自信心，提升国际知名度，以中华农耕文明优秀传统文化为主线编写而成，是我国首部用英语系统讲授中华农耕文明的一套教材。该教材立意新颖、取材颇具匠心，从我国农业的起源，如农耕五祖、原始农业的刀耕火种，到农耕思想形成和古代农书编撰；从中国传统本土农作物的培育，如五谷和中药等，到传统农业技术文化，如土壤耕作制度、农具的革新和水利灌溉工程；从农时的推算，如 24 节气和 72 物候，到农耕风俗、农耕节日、农耕艺术和农耕谚语等方面介绍了中华农耕文明的发展。

  农业院校的学生应该了解我国的农耕社会文明，这对深刻理解我国的政策方针和对今后的科研工作，有很积极的意义，尤其是学会用英语表达我国的优秀传统农耕文明，讲好中国农耕故事，至关重要。我祝愿胡家英教授团队在这个领域取得更大成绩，并希望该套教材在使用的过程中不断完善，成为一套优秀教材。

  是为序。

罗锡文

中国工程院院士、华南农业大学教授

2022 年 6 月 18 日

前 言
Preface

在绵延不断的历史长河中，炎黄子孙植五谷、饲六畜，农桑并举，耕织结合，形成了渔樵耕读、精耕细作、富国足民的优良传统，创造了上下五千年灿烂辉煌的中华文化。几千年来，中华农耕文明以其独特的文化价值和人文价值，向世界展示了中华文明的无穷魅力与风采。随着农业文明的不断发展，中华农耕文明成为中华民族一份沉甸甸的文化遗产。"耕读传家远，诗书继世长"，逐渐成为中国乡土文化的一大特色。

2021年8月，教育部印发《加强和改进涉农高校耕读教育工作方案》（以下简称《方案》）。《方案》明确提出加强学生传统农业文化教育，将耕读教育相关课程作为涉农专业学生必修课，编写中华农耕文明等教材，强化有关中华农耕文明、乡土民俗文化、乡村治理等课程教学。《中华农耕文明》（上、下册）旨在弘扬我国耕读传家优秀传统文化，加强大学生传统农业文化教育，以此促进农业特色通识教育课程体系建设，培养学生"大国三农"情怀。

本教材的编写坚持语言、文化、思维能力同步提高的教学理念，坚持课程思政，弘扬中国优秀传统文化，增强民族自信心，以内容教学法（Content-based Instruction，简称CBI）教学理念为理论依托，遵循以下三个基本原则。

一是以中华农耕文明优秀传统文化为学习主题进行语言训练的原则。本教材的编写旨在提升学生对中华农耕文明的认识和理解，并学会用英语表述，以此提升英语语言应用能力，达到用英语讲述中华农耕文明的目的，即中华农耕文明知识与语言工具兼得。

二是点面结合原则。《中华农耕文明》的编写主要从面上展示了中华农耕文明的历史面貌，从历史发展的纵向演变角度，展示农耕文明发生发展的历史脉络和标志性历史成就；《中华农耕文明》主要通过主题的拓展，从点上具体解读和展示中华农耕文明所包涵的内容及其相互关系。

三是创新原则。从内容方面，本教材比较全面地总结了中华农耕文明的相关事件和知识。从古代农学思想、精耕细作传统、农业技术文化、农业生产民俗、物候与节气文化、节庆文化、民间艺术、涉农诗词歌赋等方面概况介绍农耕文明的发展。从语言训练方面，本教材以英文为语言载体，聚焦中国优秀农耕文化知识解读，有助于中国文化的海外传播，课程思政贯穿始终。从练习的设计方面，体现读者的阅读体验和批判性思维，以独特的审美眼光指导教材的编写。从技术方面，本教材可用于线上线下混合课程，同步慕课已经全面上线。

《中华农耕文明》编写组成员主要来自东北农业大学教师团队。主编胡家英负责主题设计、编写规划等；于洋编写了上册第一章、第二章和第三章；徐虹编写了上册第四章、第五章和第六章；宋宝梅编写了下册第一章；樊绪岩编写了上册第七章、第八章，下册第二章、第三章、第四章和第五章；满盈编写了下册第六章、第七章和第八章；潘秋阳、于娜、岳欣、殷际文负责全书的校对工作。

本教材从设想到编写，从试用到出版，得到了许多同行、专家、教师和同学的支持和帮助。他们对全书的设计和编写给予了很多建议和支持。在此，我们对他们表示最衷心的感谢。

由于水平有限，缺失和不当在所难免，恳请各位同道与使用者批评与指正。

编 者

2021 年 12 月

目 录

Contents

序
前　言

第一章　农书概览
Chapter 1　Masterpieces of Ancient Agricultural Books ··············· 1
　　Text A　《齐民要术》　*Qi Min Yao Shu* ·························· 1
　　Text B　《天工开物》　*Tiangong Kaiwu* ························· 6
　　Text C　《农书》　*Nong Shu* ···································· 10

第二章　农耕风俗
Chapter 2　Farming Customs ··· 14
　　Text A　鞭打春牛　Whipping the Oxen in Early Spring ········· 14
　　Text B　龙抬头　Chinese Dragon Raises Its Head ··············· 18
　　Text C　灶王　The Kitchen God ································· 22

第三章　农耕节日
Chapter 3　Farming Festivals ·· 27
　　Text A　清明节　Qingming Festival ······························ 27
　　Text B　端午节　Dragon Boat Festival ···························· 32
　　Text C　丰收节　Chinese Farmers' Harvest Festival ············ 36

第四章　农耕谚语
Chapter 4　Agricultural Proverbs ··· 40
　　Text A　农耕谚语　About Agricultural Proverbs ················ 40
　　Text B　春、夏　Spring & Summer ······························ 45
　　Text C　秋、冬　Autumn & Winter ······························ 50

第五章　农耕艺术
Chapter 5　Farming Fine Arts ·· 56

    Text A   风筝   Kites ·· 56
    Text B   剪纸   Paper-cutting ·· 61
    Text C   皮影戏 Shadow Puppetry ·· 66

第六章 茶
Chapter 6 Tea ·· 72
    Text A   茶之识 About Tea ·· 72
    Text B   茶之史 History of Tea ··· 80
    Text C   茶之美 Beauty of Tea ·· 85

第七章 蚕桑
Chapter 7 Silkworm & Mulberry ·· 92
    Text A   蚕   Silkworm ·· 92
    Text B   桑   Mulberry ··· 99
    Text C   蚕桑文化 Culture of Silkworm and Mulberry ·· 106

第八章 稻
Chapter 8 Rice ·· 116
    Text A   稻   About Rice ··· 116
    Text B   稻产品 Main Types of Rice ·· 126
    Text C   稻文化 Rice Culture ·· 132

参考文献
Reference ·· 140

第一章 农书概览

Chapter 1 Masterpieces of Ancient Agricultural Books

Text A 《齐民要术》 Qi Min Yao Shu

Agriculture is the backbone of a China's development, fundamental to social progress and economic prosperity. For over 5000 years, the diligent and intelligent Chinese people have created a brilliant agricultural civilization, leaving behind a number of achievements that attract global attention.

Agriculture played a vital role in the development of ancient Chinese civilization. In the past centuries, both the government and civilian people in China have attached great importance to farming technology and experiences. It was under such cultural background that varieties of agricultural books came to the world in ancient China. *The Joint Catalogue of Ancient Chinese Books*, edited by Beijing Library, namely, the National Library, has recorded 643 kinds of ancient agricultural books, more than 300 of which are still safely kept so far. These books have kept a large number of valuable information and resources on traditional farming and agricultural development.

In such resourceful written documents, there are four regarded as the top extant masterpieces. They are *The Book of Fan Shengzhi*, the *Qi Min Yao Shu*, the *Chen Fu Nong Shu* and *Nong Shu* (*Wang Zhen Nong Shu*). In addition to comprehensive ones, many specialized books focus on specific agricultural practices, such as the *Leisi jing*, the oldest monograph on agricultural tools in China, and the *Classic of Tea*, the earliest introduction to tea in both China and the world.

The *Qi Min Yao Shu* (important methods to condition the people's living) is one of the oldest agrochemical treatises of China. It was written by Jia Sixie, a scholar of the short Eastern Wei period (534 AD—550 AD). He came from Yidu, modern Shandong, and was governor of the commander of Gaoyang. He had the opportunity to observe the farming activities in the regions of Jingxing, Huguan and Shangdang (all in modern Shanxi and Shaanxi) and was himself a breeder of sheep.

The *Qi Min Yao Shu* comprises 92 chapters in 10 volumes. About the author virtually nothing is known but in his foreword he at least explained that he collected quotations from all types of books, especially from older agrochemical treatises like *The Book of Fan Shengzhi* and the *Si Min Yue Ling* as well as interviews of experts on agronomy. Jia Sixie not only described how to plant and rise different kinds of crops and how to breed cattle, but also described the preparation and storage of some materials based on agrochemical products, like wine, glue, oil, fibres, dyestuffs, ink, or cooking products processes (pickling) and products like yeast, sugar and soy sauce (volume 7~9). Besides staple food (volume 1~2) he explained the cultivation of vegetables (volume 3), fruits and mulberry trees (volume 4), the latter's leaves volume used as fodder for silkworms. Volume 6 describes cattle breeding and fish-farming. In volume 10 he also described plants unpopular in central China, and his book is thus a very important source for agriculture in early China. Jia Sixie quoted from more than 150 ancient books and so preserved many fragments of texts that are otherwise lost (*The Fan Shengzhi Shu*, the *Si Min Yue Ling* or Tao Zhugong's *Yangyujing*), and also many country sayings.

The text of the book is divided into ten scrolls and 92 chapters, and records 1500-year-old Chinese agronomy, horticulture, afforestation, sericulture, animal husbandry, veterinary medicine, breeding, brewing, cooking, storage, as well as remedies for barren land. The book quoted nearly 200 ancient sources including the *Yiwu Zhi*. Important agricultural books such as *The Fan Shengzhi Shu* and the *Si Min Yue Ling* from the Han and Jin Dynasties are now lost, so future generations can only understand the operation of agriculture at the time from this book.

280 recipes are found in the text.

The *Qi Min Yao Shu* is the oldest completely surviving agricultural text of China. Jia Sixie stressed the importance of agriculture for the welfare of society and the whole state, and supported his argument by quotations from ancient masters like Ren Yan, Wang Jing, Huangfu Long, Ci Chong, Cui Shi, Huang Ba, Gong Sui and Shao Xinchen. Further proofs of this assumption come from the chapter *Hongfan* of the *Shangshu* (*The Book of Documents*) and other

Confucian Classics where the kings of the Zhou Dynasty (1054 BC—221 BC) are admonished to "appease, enrich and instruct the people". Compared with older agrochemical texts like *The Book of Fan Shengzhi* from the Han period the scope of agricultural fields is widely enlarged in the *Qi Min Yao Shu*. It includes not only the cultivation of plants, but also cattle breeding, forestry and the processing of products.

A successful farmer, according to Jia Sixie, would not only mechanically do his work, but would critically observe the seasons, weather, and the quality of the soil, in order to adapt his work to these factors. Such a method would save labour and increase yields. For the amelioration of the soil, better ploughing methods had been developed, in combination with the selection of better seeds. Jia Sixie therefore recorded 86 of various seeds in his book. For the windy and dry spring season of northern China he recommended deep-ploughing for the first cultivation of a field, but a shallow reverting of the soil in autumn, and vice versa. Between phases of cultivation, it was profitable for the preservation of moisture to level the ground and to weed out undesired grasses. Crop rotation, he says, also help to keep the fertility of the soil. Green beans planted first would enrich fertility, and had to be followed by small beans or sesame. Besides methods of sowing the author also describes different methods of plant propagation like striking, stolons, division or propping. The author seems not to have highly estimated a kind of materialization of agricultural products, as advocated by the late Han period scholar Cui Shi (the author of *Si Min Yue Ling*), but rather prefer a kind of self-subsisting farming for a single—although large—household.

Since the publication of the book, historical Chinese governments have long attached great importance to it. Since the book was spread overseas it has also often been considered a classic text to study changes in species. When Charles Darwin was researching the theory of evolution he made reference to an encyclopedia of ancient China. It is said that the book he referenced was in fact the *Qi Min Yao Shu*. The book's name *Qi Min Yao Shu* can be explained as techniques by which common people make their livelihood, but can also be explained as techniques to harness the people's livelihood.

Words & Expressions

backbone/'bækbəʊn/*n.* 脊柱；支柱
extant/ek'stænt/*adj.* 现存的；显著的
monograph/'mɒnəɑːf/*n.* 专著
treatise/'triːtɪs/*n.* 专著；论文
dyestuff/'daɪstʌf/*n.* 染料
agronomy/ə'grɒnəmi/*n.* 农学
horticulture/'hɔːtɪkʌltʃə(r)/*n.* 园艺学
sericulture/'serɪˌkʌltʃə/*n.* 养蚕
animal husbandry/'hʌzbəndri/ 畜牧业
amelioration/əˌmiːliə'reɪʃn/*n.* 改进，改善
propagation/ˌprɒpə'geɪʃn/*n.* 繁殖

Notes

1. *Qi Min Yao Shu*：《齐民要术》，中国四大古书之一。《齐民要术》大约成书于北魏末年（533—544），是北魏时期，南朝宋至梁时期，中国杰出农学家贾思勰所著的一部综合性农学著作，也是世界农学史上专著之一，是中国现存最早的一部完整的农书。

2. *Chen Fu Nong Shu*：《陈敷农书》是我国古代第一部谈论水稻栽培种植方法的农

书，宋代陈敷所著。

3. *Nong Shu*（*Wang Zhen Nong Shu*）：《王祯农书》在中国古代农学遗产中占有重要地位。它兼论了当时的中国北方农业技术和南方农业技术。

4. *Si Min Yue Ling*：《四民月令》是东汉后期崔寔创作的叙述一年例行农事活动的专书。

Reading Comprehension

I. Each piece of the following information is given in one of the paragraphs in the passage. Identify the paragraph from which the information is derived and put the corresponding number in the space provided.

(　　) 1. The *Qi Min Yao Shu* is considered to be one of the oldest agricultural books in China.

(　　) 2. In the *Qi Min Yao Shu*, Jia Sixie had ever cited from *The Book of Fan Shengzhi* and the *Si Min Yue Ling*.

(　　) 3. Agricultural fields is widely expanded in the *Qi Min Yao Shu*.

(　　) 4. Jia Sixie explains 86 of different seeds in the book.

(　　) 5. It is said that Charles Darwin made reference from the *Qi Min Yao Shu*.

II. Decide whether the statements are true (T) or false (F) according to the passage.

(　　) 1. The *Qi Min Yao Shu* is very important for agriculture in early China.

(　　) 2. Jia Sixie explains the cultivation of vegetables in volume 4.

(　　) 3. The *Qi Min Yao Shu* is the only agricultural books, so future generations can only understand the operation of agriculture from the book.

(　　) 4. In the book, the author describes numerous methods of plant propagation.

(　　) 5. Historical Chinese governments didn't focus on the book.

Language Focus

III. Complete the sentences with the correct form of the words in the table.

classic	survive	quote	divide	comprise
scope	harness	region	preserve	agronomy

1. She supports his argument by _____ from ancient masters like Ren Yan.

2. Jia Sixie quoted from more than 150 ancient books and so _____ many fragments of texts.

3. The *Qi Min Yao Shu* _____ 92 chapters in 10 volumes.

4. He had the opportunity to observe the farming activities in the _____ of Jingxing.

5. The *Qi Min Yao Shu* is one of the oldest _____ treatise of China.

6. The *Qi Min Yao Shu* is the oldest completely _____ agricultural text of China.

7. The text of the book is_____into ten scrolls and 92 chapters.

8. The_____of agricultural fields is widely enlarged in the *Qi Min Yao Shu*.

9. The book has also often been considered a_____text to study changes in species.

10. The book can also be explained as techniques to_____the people's livelihood.

IV. Match the sentences in Section A with the English translation in Section B.

Section A

1. 作者似乎不曾过高估计农业产品的市场化，正如后汉期间学者崔诗所提出的那样。

2. 由于土壤的改进，发展了更先进的耕种方法，这与选种的更优选择相结合。

3. 这本书的名字《齐民要术》可以被称为"普通人赖以生存的技术"。

4. 贾思勰认为一个成功的农民不仅仅机械地做他的工作，而且能够批判性地观察季节，天气，以及土壤的质量。

5. 关于作者的信息事实上在书中极少被提及，但是在前言中，作者解释了他从各种类型的书籍，尤其从更古老的农业文集中收集了引证。

Section B

1. About the author virtually nothing is known but in his foreword he at least explains that he collected quotations from all types of books, especially from older agronomical treatises.

2. A successful farmer, Jia Sixie says, would not only mechanically do his work, but would critically observe the seasons, weather, and the quality of the soil.

3. For the amelioration of the soil, better ploughing methods had been developed, in combination with the selection of better seeds.

4. The author seems to not have highly estimated a kind of marketization of agricultural products, as advocated by the late Han period scholar Cui Shi.

5. The book's name *Qi Min Yao Shu* can be explained as techniques by which common people make their livelihood.

V. Translate the paragraph into English.

贾思勰强调农业对于社会福利以及国家的重要性，通过引言可以看出古代学者支持他的观点。该想法的更多证据源自《尚书》中的《洪范》章节，并且在其他经籍，周朝的国王被告诫"去安抚，指导人们"。与更古老的农业著作相比，如汉朝的《氾胜之书》，在《齐民要术》中农业领域的范围已被广泛地扩大了。它不仅包含植物的种植，而且还包括牛的饲养，林业以及产品加工。

_____

_____

_____

_____

_____

Development

VI. Discuss the following questions.

1. Do you think the *Qi Min Yao Shu* is important for agriculture in China? What's the reason?

2. The reason why the *Qi Min Yao Shu* is considered to be encyclopedia of agriculture?

Text B 《天工开物》 Tiangong Kaiwu

The *Tiangong Kaiwu* (*The Exploitation of Heavenly Treasures*), is a compendium on industry, agriculture and artisanry written by the late Ming period scholar Song Yingxing (1587—?). The 18-scroll long book was written between 1634 and 1637. It was printed in 1637 by Tu Boju, during the Kangxi reign by Yang Suqing, and in 1771 by the Eisei Studio in Japan. The *Tiangong Kaiwu* is not recorded in the imperial biography of the official dynastic history *Mingshi* and was almost lost. The Japanese edition was the only surviving copy. Modern editions were published by the Zhonghua Shuju press in 1959 and the Guangdong Renmin Press in 1976. The latter includes a commentary and translation into modern Chinese by Zhong Guangyan. They have been translated into different larguages.

The term *Tiangong* first appears in the Confucian Classic, *Shangshu*, where it describes the forces of nature. The term *Kaiwu* is derived from the Classic *Yijing* (*The Book of Changes*), where it is used to refer to human processing of the products of nature. The title of the *Tiangong Kaiwu* expresses the joint forces of heaven and man to produce useful objects out of the products of nature. Man plays a central role because without him, grains would not grow.

Song Yingxing was not the typical civil official who wrote in his study without access to practical matters. Insteed he was a person interested in the reality of industrial production and manufacture and had personally observed what he described in his book. The chapters are arranged in a sociological concept that puts the five grains (wugu), i.e. agriculture, at the front, and the metals, i. e. artisanry and commerce (money), at the back of all themes. The *Tiangong Kaiwu* includes 123 excellent illustrations (the Taosheyuan edition contains 162).

The *Tiangong Kaiwu* is not only interesting because it contains a vast arrange of industrial and agricultural production methods. It furthermore provides a lot of information on where certain materials were to be found and were mainly produced. Thus it gives an excellent overview of the pronto-industrial situation of China during the early 17th century. It is very rich in content and especially valuable for the many illustrations which excellently picturize what is described in the texts. The scientific value of the *Tiangong Kaiwu* can not be overrated. It gives a picture of the high level of practical scientific knowledge of late Ming Dynasty. Arsenic, for

Chapter 1 Masterpieces of Ancient Agricultural Books

Contents

1. Naili: Grains 乃粒	10. Chuiduan: Forging and hammering 锤锻
2. Naifu: Clothing 乃服	11. Fanshi: Roasting ores 燔石
3. Zhangshi: Dyeing 彰施	12. Gaoye: Vegetable oils and fats 膏液
4. Suijing: Processing grains 粹精	13. Shaqing: Paper 杀青
5. Zuoxian: Production of salt 作咸	14. Wujin: The five metals 五金
6. Ganshi: Sugar 甘嗜	15. Jiabing: Excellent weapons 佳兵
7. Taoyan: Ceramics 陶埏	16. Danqing: Dyestoffs 丹青
8. Yezhu: Casting metals 冶铸	17. Qunie: Ferments 曲蘖
9. Zhouche: Ships and carts 舟车	18. Zhuyu: Pearls and jades 珠玉

example, was used to protect the roots of rice against rat biting and harmful vermin. The results of cross-breeding in silkworms are observed for the first time, corresponding to the Mendelian inheritance law (or the Mendel's laws of inheritance). It described looms used to produce real brocade textiles with patters woven into the structure of the cloth. In the field of metallurgy, it described how to transform the hot metal of pig iron into malleable iron by the addition of clay powder and by agitation with poles of willow wood. A mixture of both types of iron will result in steel. In mining, it described how carbon monoxide was removed through bamboo tubes, and how the galleries were stabilized against collapse by inserting a wooden shoring and wooden jacks. Concerning yeast, the *Tiangong Kaiwu* describes how "red yeast" can be applied to perishable foods to preserve it for a longer time. In the field of agriculture, it is described how important water was for the growing of rice. The *Tiangong Kaiwu* is mainly based on real experience and less on cosmological speculations, as was often the case in earlier writings. It therefore also provides the reader with a lot of practical information, including measurements and proportions, like 80% of ox fat and 20% of wax for creating models for casting. Water power was the most effective way of watering field, because they could operate day and night, while human power was only able to fulfil a twentieth of the work a waterwheel could provide, an ox the tenth part of it.

It was also of importance which kind of millstone was used. The northern "cold stone" would yield 80% more of flower than other stones. The production of silk yarn cost eight times the time—and the price—of fresh reel silk. The yield in oil of sesame was higher than that of hemp, and it could not only be used in the kitchen, but the by-products were also useful a fertilizers for fields. It is described, where certain raw materials had to be transported from, like hard clay from and soft clay from Qimen that were brought by ship to the porcelain kilns at Jingdezhen, or tung oil from Hebei and Henan that was brought to Huizhou as a surrogate for the expensive pine resin. Song Yingxing also explains why gold was not used to produce coins because it was too precious to be used in daily life. For this purpose, the cheap copper coins were of great value. He observes at the same time that there was not sufficient silver in circulation to supply the monetary markets. Transport was of important means for the distribution of goods among the empire. Tools of transport were therefore a crucial means for the distribution of wealth. Overseas trade is also dealt with in the chapter on ships.

The *Tiangong Kaiwu* is one of the most important early books on Chinese science and technology. With its wide range of topics described, it can serve as an encyclopedia on early modern crafts and industry in China. Later books therefore often quoted text and copied the illustrations in the *Tiangong Kaiwu*, like the Qing period (1644—1911) encyclopedia *Gujin Tushu Jicheng*, the agricultural book *Shoushi Tongkao*, Wu Qijun's *Diannan Kuangchan tulue* (on mining in Yunnan), *Zhiwu Mingshi Tukao* (on plants and their economical use), Li Yueyun's *Gewu Zhongfa*, or Wei Jiesuo's *Cansang Cuibian* (on silkworm breeding).

Modern scholars were likewise highly interested in the *Tiangong Kaiwu*. There were several prints made during the early 20th century. Liang Qichao recognized the *Tiangong Kaiwu*, along with the *Xu Xiake Youji*, as one of the most important books of the last few centuries. Ding Wenjiang praised Song Yingxing's vast knowledge and his excellent power of observation. There are, nevertheless, some erroneous traditional ways of thought reflected in the *Tiangong Kaiwu*, the most outstanding of which might be the belief that coal grew again inside the mountain some 30 years after the layers had been exploited. In 1952 the first modern print of the *Tiangong Kaiwu* was made, based on the edition of the Mohai Studio of Master Li of Ningbo. In 1959 a facsimile was reprinted by the Shanghai Zhonghua Shuju Press. The *Tiangong Kaiwu* is included in the reprint series *Xiyongxuan Congshu* and *Zhongguo Gudai Keji Tulu Congbian*, but not in the *Siku Quanshu*. There is a study on the book by the 20th century scholar Pan Jixing, the *Tiangong Kaiwu Daodu*.

Words & Expressions

compendium/kəmˈpendiəm/*n*. 概略；汇编
commentary/ˈkɒmənt(ə)ri/*n*. 注释；评论
artisanry/ˈɑːtɪzənrɪ/*n*. 手工艺
arsenic/ˈɑːsnɪk/*n*. 砷；砒霜
vermin/ˈvɜːmɪn/*n*. 害虫
brocade/brəˈkeɪd/*n*. 织锦
metallurgy/məˈtælədʒi/*n*. 冶金
yeast/jiːst/*n*. 酵母
perishable/ˈperɪʃəb(ə)l/*adj*. 易腐烂的；短暂的
sesame/ˈsesəmi/*n*. 芝麻
hemp/hemp/*n*. 大麻
surrogate/ˈsʌrəgət/*adj*. 代替的
resin/ˈrezɪn/*n*. 树脂

copper/'kɒpə(r)/*n.* 铜
facsimile/fæk'sɪməli/*n.* 传真

Notes

1. *Tiangong Kaiwu*：《天工开物》由明代著名科学家宋应星初刊于 1637 年（明崇祯十年丁丑），共三卷十八篇，全书收录了农业、手工业，诸如机械、砖瓦、陶瓷、硫黄、烛、纸、兵器、火药、纺织、染色、制盐、采煤、榨油等生产技术。《天工开物》是世界上第一部关于农业和手工业生产的综合性著作，是中国古代一部综合性的科学技术著作，外国学者称它为"中国 17 世纪的工艺百科全书"。

2. *Mingshi*：《明史》是二十四史中的最后一部，共 332 卷。它是一部纪传体断代史，记载了自 1368 年（明太祖朱元璋洪武元年）至明思宗朱由检 1644 年（崇祯十七年）276 年的历史。

3. *Shangshu (The Book of Documents)*：《尚书》又称《书》《书经》，是我国第一部上古历史文件和部分追述古代事迹著作的汇编，是儒家五经之一。

4. *Yijing (The Book of Changes)*：易经，是阐述天地世间万象变化的古老经典，是博大精深的辩证法哲学书。包括《连山》《归藏》《周易》三部易书，其中《连山》《归藏》已经失传，现存于世的只有《周易》。

5. *Gujin Tushu Jicheng*：《古今图书集成》原名《古今图书汇编》，全书共 10000 卷，采撷广博，内容非常丰富，上至天文、下至地理，中有人类、禽兽、昆虫，乃至文学、乐律等，包罗万象。

Reading Comprehension

Ⅰ. **Each piece of the following information is given in one of the paragraphs in the passage. Identify the paragraph from which the information is derived and put the corresponding number in the space provided.**

(　　) 1. The *Tiangong Kaiwu* is not recorded in the imperial biography of the official dynastic history *Mingshi* and was almost lost.

(　　) 2. It is very rich in content and especially valuable for the many illustrations which excellently picturize what is described in the texts.

(　　) 3. There were several prints made during the early 20th century.

(　　) 4. The title of the *Tiangong Kaiwu* expresses the joint forces of Heaven and man to produce useful objects out of the products of nature.

(　　) 5. The *Tiangong Kaiwu* includes 123 excellent illustrations.

Ⅱ. **Decide whether the statements are true (T) or false (F) according to the passage.**

(　　) 1. The 18-volume long book was written between 1368 and 1637.

(　　) 2. The term "kaiwu" is derived from the Confucian Classic *Shangshu (The Book of Documents)*, where it is used to refer to human processing of the products of nature.

(　　) 3. Arsenic was used to protect the roots of rice against rat biting and harmful vermin.

(　　) 4. Song Yingxing was the typical civil official who wrote in his study without access to practical matters.

(　　) 5. The *Tiangong Kaiwu* is not included in the *Siku Quanshu*.

III. Discuss the following questions.

1. When did the Modern editions of the *Tiangong Kaiwu* published? And by who?
2. Please write down your brief comments on the importance of the *Tiangong Kaiwu*.

Text C 《农书》 Nong Shu

Wang Zhen (1290—1333) was a Chinese mechanical engineer, agronomist, inventor, writer, and politician of the Yuan Dynasty. He was one of the early innovators of the wooden movable type-printing technology. His illustrated agricultural treatise was also one of the most advanced of his age, covering a wide range of equipment and technologies available in the late 13th and early 14th century.

Wang Zhen was born in Shandong Province, and spent many years as an official of both Anhui and Jiangxi Provinces. From 1290 to 1301, he was a magistrate for Jingde, Anhui Province, where he was a pioneer of the use of wooden movable type printing; the wooden movable type was described in Wang Zhen's publication of 1313, known as the *Nong Shu*, or *The Book of Agriculture*. Although the title describes the main focus of the work, it incorporated much more information on a wide variety of subjects that was not limited to the scope of agriculture. Wang's *Nong Shu* of 1313 was a very important medieval treatise outlining the application and use of the various Chinese sciences, technologies, and agricultural practices. From water powered bellows to movable type printing, it is considered a descriptive masterpiece on contemporary medieval Chinese technology.

Wang wrote the masterpiece *Nong Shu* for many practical reasons, but also as a means to aid and support destitute rural farmers in China looking for means to improve their economic livelihoods in the face of poverty and oppression during the Yuan period. Although the previous Song Dynasty was a period of high Chinese culture and relative economic and agricultural stability, the conquering Mongol rulers of the Yuan Dynasty thoroughly damaged the economic and agricultural base of China during the conquest of it. Hence, a book such as the *Nong Shu* could help rural farmers maximize efficiency of producing yields and they could learn how to use various agricultural tools to aid their daily lives. However, it was not intended to be read by rural farmers (who were largely illiterate), but local officials who desired to research the best agricultural methods currently available that the peasants otherwise would know little of.

The *Nong Shu* was an incredibly long book even for its own time, which had over 110000 written Chinese characters. However, this was only slightly larger than the early medieval Chinese agricultural treatise the *Qi Min Yao Shu* written by Jia Sixia in 535, which had slightly over 100000 written Chinese characters.

Contents

1. Comprehensive prescriptions for agriculture and sericulture: 农业和蚕桑综合处方
2. Treatise on the Hundred Grains: 百粮论
3. Cereals (including legumes, hemp, and sesame): 谷物（包括豆类，大麻和芝麻）
4. Cucurbits and green vegetables: 葫芦和绿色蔬菜
5. Fruits: 水果
6. Bamboos and miscellaneous (including ramie, cotton, tea, dye plants, etc.): 竹子和其他种类（包括麻，棉花，茶，染料植物等）
7. Illustrated Treatise on Agricultural Implements: 关于农具的图解说明
8. Field systems: 大田制度
9. Agricultural tools: 农业工具
10. Wicker and basket ware: 柳条篮用品
11. Food-processing equipment and grain storage: 食品加工设备和谷物储存
12. Ceremonial vessels, transport: 礼仪船，运输
13. Irrigation equipment, water-powered mills, etc.: 灌溉设备，水力磨坊等
14. Special implements for wheat: 小麦专用工具
15. Sericulture and textile production: 蚕桑和纺织品生产

The main focus of the *Nong Shu* written by Wang was the realm of Chinese agriculture, his book listed and described an enormous catalogue of agricultural tools and implements used in the past and in his own day. Furthermore, Wang incorporated a systematic usage of illustrated pictures in his book to accompany every piece of farming equipment described. Wang also created an agricultural calendrical diagram in the form of a circle, which included the Heavenly Stems, the Earthly Branches, the four seasons, twelve months, twenty-four solar terms, seventy-two five-day periods, with each sequence of agricultural tasks and the natural phenomena which signal for their necessity, stellar configurations, phenology, and the sequence of agricultural production.

Amongst the various contemporary agricultural practices mentioned in the *Nong Shu*, Wang listed and described the use of ploughing, sowing, irrigation, cultivation of mulberries, etc, it listed and described many of the various foodstuffs and products of the many regions of China. The book outlined the use of not only agricultural tools, but food-processing, irrigation equipment, different types of fields, ceremonial vessels, various types of grain storage, carts, boats, mechanical devices, and textile machinery used in many applications. For example, one of the many devices described and illustrated in drawing is a large mechanical milling plant operated by the motive power of oxen, with an enormous rotating geared wheel engaging the toothed gears of eight different mills surrounding it. With great interest to sinologist historians,

Wang also outlined the difference between the agricultural technology of Northern China and that of Southern China; the main characteristic of agricultural technology of the north was technical applications fit for predominantly dry land cultivation, while intensified irrigation cultivation was more suitable for Southern China. Furthermore, Wang used his treatise as means to spread knowledge in support of certain agricultural practices or technologies found exclusively in either south or north that could benefit the other, if only they were more widely known, such as the southern hand-harrow used for weeding in the south, yet virtually unknown in the north.

Wang made some technical innovations in the book, one of which is the movable type printing. In improving movable type printing, Wang mentioned an alternative method of baking porcelain printing type with earthenware frame in order to make whole blocks. Wang is best known for his usage of wooden movable type while he was a magistrate of Jingde in Anhui province from 1290 to 1301. His main contribution was improving the speed of typesetting with simple mechanical devices, along with the complex, systematic arrangement of wooden movable types.

Words & Expressions

magistrate/'mædʒɪstreɪt/ *n.* 地方法官
destitute/'destɪtjuːt/ *adj.* 贫困的
irrigation/ˌɪrɪ'ɡeɪʃn/ *n.* 灌溉
vessel/'vesəl/ *n.* 容器
sinologist/saɪ'nɒlədʒɪst; sɪ'nɒlədʒɪst/ *n.* 汉学家
earthenware/'ɜːθnweə(r)/ *n.* 陶器

Notes

1. *Nong Shu*：《农书》在中国古代农学遗产中占有重要地位。它兼论中国北方农业技术和中国南方农业技术。由于中国古代劳动人民积累了数千年的耕作经验，留下了丰富的农学著作。先秦诸书中多含有农学篇章，《农书》在前人著作基础上，第一次对所谓的广义农业生产知识作了较全面系统的论述，提出中国农学的传统体系。

2. Wang zheng also created an agricultural calendrical diagram in the form of a circle, which included the Heavenly Stems, the Earthly Branches, the four seasons, twelve months, twenty-four solar terms, seventy-two five-day periods, with each sequence of agricultural tasks and the natural phenomena which signal for their necessity, stellar configurations, phenology, and the sequence of agricultural production.
王祯还创建了一个圆形的农业历法，包括天干、地支、四季、十二月、二十四节气、七十二候，标明了每个农业任务的序列和表明其必要性的自然现象，星宿配置，物候和农业生产顺序。

第一章 农书概览

Chapter 1 Masterpieces of Ancient Agricultural Books

Reading Comprehension

I. Each piece of the following information is given in one of the paragraphs in the passage. Identify the paragraph from which the information is derived and put the corresponding number in the space provided.

(   ) 1. Wang Zhen was one of the early innovators of the wooden movable type printing technology.

(   ) 2. From 1290 to 1301, Wang Zhen was a magistrate for Jingde, Anhui Province.

(   ) 3. Wang Zhen incorporated a systematic usage of illustrated pictures in his book to accompany every piece of farming equipment described.

(   ) 4. Wang Zhen listed and described the use of ploughing, sowing, irrigation, cultivation of mulberries, etc. in *Nong Shu*.

(   ) 5. Wang made some technical innovations in the book, one of which is the movable type printing.

II. Decide whether the statements are true (T) or false (F) according to the passage.

(   ) 1. Wang's *Nong Shu* of 1313 was a very important medieval treatise outlining the application and use of the various Chinese sciences, technologies, and agricultural practices.

(   ) 2. The conquering Mongol rulers of the Ming Dynasty thoroughly damaged the economic and agricultural base of China.

(   ) 3. The main focus of the *Nong Shu* written by Wang Zhen was the realm of Chinese agriculture.

(   ) 4. Wang Zhen also created an agricultural calendrical diagram in the form of a square, which included the Heavenly Stems, the Earthly Branches, the four seasons, twelve months, 24 solar terms, etc.

(   ) 5. Wang Zhen is best known for his usage of wooden movable type while he was a magistrate of Jingde in Jiangxi Province from 1290 to 1301.

Development

III. Discuss the following questions.

1. Except the main focus of *Nong Shu* in the realm of Chinese agriculture, what does Wang Zhen describe (just list one point)?

2. What is the difference between the agricultural technology of Northern China and that of Southern China described in Wang Zhen's *Nong Shu*?

第二章 农耕风俗
Chapter 2 Farming Customs

鞭打春牛
Whipping the Oxen in Early Spring

China is an agricultural country, and the Chinese people attach great importance to welcoming spring on Spring Equinox Day. It even became a national festival for the people to welcome spring by whipping the oxen during the Emperor Qianlong's (1711—1799) reign during the Qing Dynasty.

The custom to whip the oxen in early spring falls into two kinds: one is an imitation of whipping a real ox in the public and the other reflects the notion of such a custom putting up a picture or a similar thing which portrays the general activities involved in the custom.

According to the historical records of the *Ji'nan Prefecture Annals*, officials whipped the oxen three times with colored sticks on Spring Equinox Day, encouraging the people to farm and plant. The three whips had different meanings: the first whip meant seasonable weather for crop raising, the second symbolized the country flourishing and people living in peace, and the third symbolized the mercy of the emperors reaching into the farthest corners of the earth.

The custom stems from an early Qin Dynasty legend. In ancient China, the chief of Dong Yi Nationality and his people moved to the lower reaches of the Yellow River and he asked his people to convert their nomadic way of life to life as settled farmers. Goumang, his son was assigned to manage the conversion. Goumang collected some reed just before the end of the lashing winter days and burned them. The ashes were stuffed into a bamboo tube. And then he waited beside the tube. When the very moment the spring came, the ashes in the bamboo tube rose and floated in the air, and the spring was thought to have arrived. Goumang gave timely orders that everybody plough the fields so as to make things ready for sowing.

As humans, his people understood the situation, but the oxen that were expected to help to plough the fields were still in deep winter sleep and refused to get busy. Some people suggested to whip them to wake them up. Goumang disagreed the idea, saying that the oxen were to help us humans as friends and they should not be ill-treated. He thought that mere intimidation would suffice. He then, asked his people to mould clay oxen to be whipped. The cracking noise startled the sleeping real oxen. When they realized what was going on around them, they all became fully awoke and went about their business under the command of the farmers without hesitation. Because of the timely ploughing and seeding, a bumper harvest was secured. The people who used to be nomads all took to farming happily. This practice gradually became a set of rule for people to judge the seasons and decided the right time to plough and sow.

In the Zhou Dynasty, with the widespread development of the agricultural economy, the custom to whip the oxen in early spring became an official ceremony. Three days before every beginning of the spring, the emperor of the Zhou Dynasty would begin to eat no meat and take special baths to get prepared for the ceremony. When the day arrived emperor would head his officials and officers to the eastern suburbs to see in the spring. The way to judge the coming of spring remained basical the same as what Goumang did (later down replaced ashes). Besides, artificial life-sized oxen which were made before hand were placed there. As soon as the exact arrival of spring was there, the fake oxen were beaten to mean the commencement of ploughing and seeding in the field. In the Tang and Song Dynasties, such set of ceremony developed into a nationwide activity both for the ruling and working classes at the same time.

Whipping oxen could be a very lively occasion. As usual the chief executive would take the lead in whipping the oxen with a gorgeously ornamented whip and the others took turns according to their ranks, whipping the oxen till the clay oxen were broken into pieces. They believed that the pieces had magic power. By throwing them into the pads a good harvest would be a sure thing. There could also be paper oxen inside the bellies of which the five kinds of grain crops were stuffed. When the paper oxen were torn open with the whipping, the five cereals would burst out, which was taken as the indication of bumper crop. In the later Qing Dynasty, the official ceremony came to an end, the peasants themselves got organized for the ceremony, but they changed something in and added something to the big annual occasion.

As mentioned earlier, there was the other kind, different in form, but similar in purpose. That is the picture portraying the custom to whip the oxen, which means the best wishes for a good harvest. In the picture, there was always a cowboy with a willow to resemble the whip and an ox. Such picture would be available towards the end of the Spring Festival. On the picture there was always something written as auspicious words. This kind of custom is still popular in the Chinese countryside.

Words & Expressions

reign /reɪn/ n. （君主）在位时期，统治时期；领导期，任期；支配期，极盛期
flourish/ˈflʌrɪʃ/ v. 繁荣，昌盛；挥动；（植物或动物）长势好，茁壮成长
nomadic /nəʊˈmædɪk/ adj. 游牧的；流浪的
suffice /səˈfaɪs/ v. 足够，足以；满足…的需求；有能力
mould /məʊld/ v. 使…成形，用模子制作，浇铸；影响，塑造
commencement /kəˈmensmənt/ n. 开始，开端
resemble/rɪˈzemb(ə)l/ v. 像，与…相似
auspicious /ɔːˈspɪʃəs/ adj. 有助于成功的，有利的；吉利的，吉兆的

Notes

Whipping the oxen in early spring: 鞭打春牛的活动起源于先秦时的历史传说。相传古代东夷族首领率民迁居黄河下游，要大家放弃游牧改学耕作，并派他的儿子句芒管理这项事业。句芒在寒冬即将逝去前，采河边葭草烧成灰烬，放在竹管内，然后守候在竹管旁。到了冬尽春来的那一瞬间，竹管内的草灰便浮扬起来，标志着春天降临了。于是句芒下令大家一起翻土田，准备播种。人都能理解句芒的命令，可是要帮人犁田的老牛却仍沉浸在"冬眠"的甜睡中，懒得爬起来干活。有人建议把它们抽醒。但是句芒不同意，说牛是我们的帮手，不许虐待，吓唬吓唬就行了。于是他让人们用泥土捏制成牛的形状，然后对之鞭打。鞭响声惊醒了酣睡的老牛，一看在地上睡觉的同类正在挨抽，吓得站起身来，乖乖地听人指挥，下地干活去了。由于按时耕作，当年又获得了好收成，原先以畜牧为生的人们都乐于从事农业了。而这种看灰立春、鞭打土牛的习俗也逐渐成为人们判断时令、及时耕作的定规。

Reading Comprehension

I. Each piece of the following information is given in one of the paragraphs in the passage. Identify the paragraph from which the information is derived and put the corresponding number in the space provided.

(   ) 1. It even became a national festival for the people to welcome spring by whipping the oxen during the Emperor Qianlong's reign during the Qing Dynasty.

(   ) 2. According to the historical records, officials whipped the oxen three times with colored sticks on Spring Equinox Day, encouraging the people to farm and plant.

(   ) 3. When the very moment the spring came, the ashes in the bamboo tube rose and floated in the air, and the spring was thought to have arrived.

(   ) 4. When they realized what was going on around them, they all became fully awoke and went about their business under the command of the farmers without hesitation.

(   ) 5. That is the picture portraying the custom to whip the oxen, which means the best wishes for a good harvest.

II. Decide whether the statements are true (T) or false (F) according to the passage.

(　　) 1. The chief of Dong Yi Nationality asked his people to convert life as settled farmers to the nomadic way of life.

(　　) 2. Goumang agreed the idea to whip the oxen in deep winter sleep to wake them up.

(　　) 3. In the Zhou Dynasty, with the agricultural economy got widely developed, the custom to whip the oxen in early spring became an official ceremony.

(　　) 4. Nine days before every beginning of the spring, the emperor of the Zhou Dynasty would begin to eat no meat and take special baths to get prepared for the ceremony.

(　　) 5. In the Tang and Song Dynasties, such set of ceremony developed into a nationwide activity both for the ruling and working classes at the same time.

Language Focus

III. Complete the sentences with the correct form of the words in the table.

commence	flourish	gorgeous	nomad	auspicious
intimidate	cereal	mould	crack	bumper

1. The three whips had different meanings: the second symbolized the country _____ and people living in peace.

2. In ancient China, the chief of Dong Yi Nationality asked his people to convert their _____ way of life to life as settled farmers.

3. He thought that mere _____ would suffice.

4. He then, asked his people to _____ clay oxen to be whipped.

5. Because of the timely ploughing and seeding, a _____ harvest was secured.

6. The _____ noise startled the sleeping real oxen.

7. As soon as the exact arrival of spring was there, the fake oxen were beaten to mean the _____ of ploughing and seeding in the field.

8. As usual the chief executive would take the lead in whipping the oxen with a _____ ornamented whip and others took turns according to their ranks.

9. When the paper oxen were torn open with the whipping, the five _____ would burst out.

10. On the picture there was always something written as _____ words.

IV. Match the sentences in Section A with the English translation in Section B.

Section A

1. 当确认已迎来春天后，便用鞭子抽打土牛，表示督催春耕。
2. 这种看灰立春、鞭打土牛的习俗也逐渐成为人们判断时令、及时耕作的定规。
3. 张贴鞭牛的风俗画像，表达了祈求丰收的美好愿望。

4. 鞭打春牛的习俗有两种形式：其一是模仿鞭打真牛；其二是对这一活动所含意义的概括和表达——张贴反映这一风俗的图像。

Section B

1. The custom to whip the oxen in early spring falls into two kinds: one kind is an imitation of whipping a real ox in the public. The other reflects the notion of such a custom putting up a picture or a similar thing which portrays the general activities involved in the custom.

2. This practice gradually became a set of rule for people to judge the seasons and decided the right time to plough and sow.

3. As soon as the exact arrival of spring was there, the fake oxen were beaten to mean the commencement of ploughing and seeding in the field.

4. That is the picture portraying the custom to whip the oxen, which is to mean the best wishes for a good harvest.

V. Translate the paragraph into Chinese.

Whipping oxen could be a very lively occasion. As usual the chief executive would take the lead in whipping the oxen with a gorgeously ornamented whip and the others took turns according to their ranks, whipping the oxen till the clay oxen were broken into pieces. They believed that the pieces had magic power. By throwing them into the pads a good harvest would be a sure thing. There could also be paper oxen inside the bellies of which the five kinds of grain crops were stuffed. When the paper oxen were torn open with the whipping, the five cereals would burst out, which was taken as the indication of bumper crop.

_____
_____
_____
_____
_____

VI. Discuss the following questions.

1. How many times were the oxen whipped? What did they mean?
2. What does whipping the oxen in early spring stem from?

Text B 龙抬头
Chinese Dragon Raises Its Head

A Chinese common proverb goes, "Er yue er, long tai tou", which means the second day of the second month of the Lunar calendar is the time the dragon awakens. Traditionally, it is the Dragon Day. It is observed not only by Han people (the majority nationality in China), but by more than ten minority nationalities as well, and therefore has substantial content.

The day was found recorded as early as the Tang and the Song Dynasties. Yet the activities done to celebrate such a day during that time were excursions in spring, treading on the grass, picking edible wild herbs. The belief that the dragon awakens on the second day of the second month of the Chinese lunar calendar can be traced back to the ancient understanding of the Dragon (long). In *Explaining and Elaborating Characters* or *Shuowen Jiezi* (a classic Chinese academic work in which the meanings of Chinese characters are glossed), the word Dragon (long) is described as the master creature of all the creatures with scale and shell, and of the vernal equinox, it soars to the heaven... Before the Spring Equinox was the time of the waking of insects according to Chinese lunar calendar which means the startling of the insects and their scattering here and there. The dragon belongs to the insects family and therefore can be no exception when other insects are startled. Before the Han Dynasty the dragon was believed to in charge of clouds and rains. Usually the early spring in China had not much rain at all, when the fields of crop were in desperate want of rain. So it was vitally important for people to expect the dragon's soaring into the heaven at night and giving people the rains they desired.

There has long been a popular folktale about the originality of the custom. When Wu Zetian, the Empress during the Tang Dynasty, also the first and only Empress Regnant in Chinese history, coined herself the Chinese character (zhao in standard Chinese phonetic alphabet means the sun and the moon that give light to the earth) to illustrate her the greatness. The Jade Emperor (a Chinese mythological figure believed to be the Supreme Emperor in the Heaven) was irritated thinking that it was too arrogant of the Empress to compare herself to the sun, the moon and the one who gave light to the earth, because the Jade Emperor was widely recognized as the greatest emperor taking care of everything on earth in Chinese mythology. The Jade Emperor decided to show his power and punish the empress by asking a minor god to deliver his order to the four dragons living in the four seas that there be no rain for the earth for three years. The order made the four dragons quite happy because they would stop giving rains and therefore have time enough to enjoy themselves. But the people on the earth began to suffer from a terrible lack of water. One of the four dragons in the one west sea had a son who was very kind. When he learned the situation, his heart went out to the living creatures and plants on the earth. Regardless of the Jade Emperor's order, he secretly gave some rain onto the earth. The Jade Emperor became outraged at this defiance, so he had the son of the west sea dragon put under the bottom of a huge mountain as a penalty. And on the mountain side he had a boar set on which his order was engraved: "Unless a gold bean can bloom, the dragon should not be set free and there should be no rain." No dragon since dared to do anything against the orders anymore. People on the earth were almost hopeless. But they never give in. One day, when someone came across a corn field, he hit upon an idea, namely the corn seed looked very much like a gold bean and it also bore a strong resemblance to a gold bean in bloom as popped corns would look like. So every family began to pop corns and burns incense to send message to the Heaven, and at the same time they shouted: "The gold beans are in bloom." Upon hearing the clamor, and seeing the popped corn seeds in the courtyards of every house on earth, the Jade Emperor felt it was hard for him not to keep his word. There immediately was a heavy rain onto the earth. And it so happened that the day there was rain again for the earth was the second day of second month of the lunar calendar.

The most popular custom on the Dragon Heads-raising Day is pepole have their hair cut. Dragon is highly esteemed for its dignity and power for good. It is thought to be auspicious to have hair cut on the Dragon Heads-raising Day. Luck and opportunities will always knock you in the year. So, on that day, barbershops' businesses are prospering and full of customers. According to the Chinese tradition, it's bad luck to have hair cut during the first lunar month. As the Chinese saying goes "If you have your hair cut in the first lunar month, your uncle will die". So, people usually have their hair cut before the first lunar month and wait to the Dragon Heads-raising Day to cut again.

The most common food for celebrating the festival are popcorns, pancakes, noodles, dumplings, fired soy beans and pig's head. People in different areas have different traditions about the food on the day. In Beijing, people eat Lvdagunr (Glutinous Rice Rolls with Sweet Bean Flour) and spring pancakes on the day.

In Shanxi, people like to eat fried dough twists and pancakes. In Shandong, fried soy beans, noodles and dumplings are the festival food. In Fuzhou, the salted porridge made of glutinous rice, celery, scallion, garlic, fry dried shrimps and shredded meat is eaten.

To be auspicious, what people eat on the Dragon Heads-raising Day is usually renamed after parts of the dragon. Eating dumplings is called eating "dragon's ears," spring pancakes are called "dragon's scales," rice is called "dragon's son", wontons are "dragon's eyes", pancake is the "dragon scale", noodles are "dragon beard noodles", and fried dough twists are "dragon's bones", etc. These show people's hope to be blessed with favorable weather and bumper grain harvest by the dragon.

In some places people go to suburb for relaxing on the day. Also some people worship to the dragon or earth god with the hope that there would be rains helping the agriculture.

In some rural areas, the day is also called the daughters'day. On the day, the married daughters would come home and stay for some days to accompany their parents. Later, they will come back to help with crops planting.

Words & Expressions

excursion/ɪk'skɜːʃn/ *n.* 短途旅行，远足；涉猎；移动；游览团，远足队；离题；偏移，偏差

scatter /'skætə(r)/ v. 撒，播撒；（使）散开，（使）散布在各处
regnant /'regnənt/ adj. 在位的，统治的；占优势（或主导）的；流行的，广泛的
defiance /dɪ'faɪəns/ n. 违抗，蔑视
engrave /ɪn'greɪv/ v. 雕刻（文字，图案）；铭刻在（记忆，脑海）中
resemblance /rɪ'zembləns/ n. 相似，相像；相似点，相似之处；相似物
scallion /'skæliən/ n. 青葱，冬葱；韭葱

Notes

1. Chinese Dragon Raises Its Head：关于"龙抬头"的习俗起源，有一则民间故事至今很流行。传说大唐时武则天做了皇帝，她也是中国历史上唯一的女皇帝。她为自己制造了"瞾"字作"圣讳"（瞾字意为日月当空，普照人间）。这把天上的玉帝惹恼了，他认为武则天目中无人，自比日月，而玉帝才是治理人间最伟大的帝王啊！玉帝一发火，决定让他手下的一名神仙向四海龙王传旨：三年之内，不得向人间降水！玉帝有旨，龙王们乐得休假玩耍，老百姓却因缺雨水而吃尽了苦头。四海龙王之一的西海龙王的儿子非常善良，他得知人间的这等惨景，不禁动了恻隐之心。他不顾玉帝的旨意，偷偷降水人间。玉帝被气得七窍生烟，他下令将西海龙王之子压于大山底下作为惩罚，并在山前立了块碑，上面刻着：若想翻身回天，除非金豆开花。从此后，四海龙王再不敢抗旨行雨了。为了寻找金豆开花，老百姓焦急万分，但却从来没有放弃。一天，有人恰巧经过玉米地，他忽来灵感，金黄的玉米就像金豆，把它炒一炒开了花，就是如金豆开花一般。于是家家户户开始爆炒起玉米来，同时设案焚香，并齐声高喊："金豆开花了！"听到人间的吵闹，同时看到家家户户摆放的被炒开花的玉米玉帝也不便食言了。马上，又有雨降临人间，而恰巧再次降水的那天是农历的二月初二。

2. *Explaining and Elaborating Characters* or *Shuowen Jiezi*：《说文解字》，简称《说文》，作者是东汉的经学家、文字学家许慎。《说文解字》成书于汉和帝 100 年（永元十二年）到安帝 121 年（建光元年）。许慎根据文字的形体，创立 540 个部首，将 9353 字分别归入 540 部。540 部又据形系联归并为十四大类。字典正文就按这十四大类分为十四篇，卷末叙目别为一篇，全书共有十五篇，其中包括序目一卷。许慎在《说文解字》中系统地阐述了汉字的造字规律——六书。

Reading Comprehension

I. **Each piece of the following information is given in one of the paragraphs in the passage. Identify the paragraph from which the information is derived and put the corresponding number in the space provided.**

(　　) 1. Dragon Day is observed not only by Han people, but by more than ten minority nationalities as well, and therefore has substantial content.

(　　) 2. So it was vitally important for people to expect the dragon's soaring into the heaven at night and giving people the rains they desired.

(　　) 3. Upon hearing the clamor, and seeing the popped corn seeds in the courtyards of every house on earth, the Jade Emperor felt it was hard for him not to keep his word.

(   ) 4. The most popular custom on the Dragon Heads-raising Day is people have their hair cut.

(   ) 5. In some rural areas, the day is also called the daughters' day.

II. Decide whether the statements are true (T) or false (F) according to the passage.

(   ) 1. The day was found recorded as early as the Tang Dynasty.

(   ) 2. Before the Han Dynasty the dragon was believed to in charge of clouds and rains.

(   ) 3. The Jade Emperor became outraged at this defiance, so he had the son of the east sea dragon put under the bottom of a huge mountain as a penalty.

(   ) 4. According to the Chinese tradition, it's bad luck to have hair cut during the first lunar month.

(   ) 5. To be auspicious, what people eat on the Dragon Heads-raising Day is usually renamed after parts of the dragon.

III. Discuss the following questions.

1. Why did the ancient people long the dragon's soaring?

2. What are the food to celebrate this festival?

Text C 灶王 / The Kitchen God

Amidst the clamor of preparations for the Lunar New Year, time until the 23rd day of the 12th lunar month (in the north) or the 24th (in the south), when the time came to make offerings to the Kitchen God (Zaowangye). It was widely believed that the Kitchen God ascended to heaven on one of these two days to make his annual report on the behavior of the members of each house-hold.

In ancient China the Kitchen God commanded very high prestige among people. He was worshipped as the inventor of fire. When, much later, a special god of fire appeared in the Chinese pantheon, he was worshipped as a family god and the protector of the hearth.

The degree of respect accorded the Kitchen God was unusual in that people used to burn candles before his shrine on the first and 15th days of each month, rather than on one festival only during the year the case with most other gods. In addition all the cooks in Beijing would go to the Temple of the Kitchen God to honor their patron on the third day of the eighth lunar month, which was said to be his birthday.

Each household had s shrine for the Kitchen God in a corner on the back wall behind the hearth. It was usually blackened with smoke and frequently filled with cockroaches, which were referred to as "the horses of the god". These shrines could be made out of a variety of materials, including bamboo, wood and paper. Inside each one was pasted a picture of the Kitchen God in one of several forms. He was sometimes portrayed in a sitting position beside a fully harnessed horse sometimes as a young man with a recording tablet in hand on which he wrote the things that he must report to heaven and sometimes as an old man seated next to his aged wife. Those families that were too poor to buy such paintings, would paste a small square of red paper on the god's shrine instead. Written on the paper were the names of the god his title, and a special apology from the family, as follows:

Oh, Kitchen God, oh, Kitchen God,
Here is a bowl of water and three incense sticks.
Our life this past year was not so good,
Perhaps next year we'll offer you Manchurian sugar!

The worship of the Kitchen God dates back over 2000 years. *The Rites of Zhou*, a book of the Confucian school that records the decrees and regulations of both Western Zhou Dynasty and the Warring States period states: Zhu Rong, the son of Zhuan Xu and grandson of the Yellow Emperor, had been in charge of fire in life and was ordained the God of Kitchen after death. During the Zhou period, wealthy families placed oblations for him on their hearths. The philosophical book of Taoism, *Huai Nan Zi*, which was completed in the Western Han Dynasty contains the following passage: "The Yellow Emperor invented the hearth and was worshipped as the Kitchen God after his death." The Kitchen God is thus placed on the same footing as the Yellow Emperor who is considered as the common ancestor of the Chinese people. The actual identity of the Kitchen God has been the subject of numerous interpretations over the course of time. Owing perhaps to the fact that older women did most of the cooking, people at one time believed that the Kitchen God was an old lady. Later on the belief that the god was a young lady became prevalent. Finally the most widely accepted version came to the conclusion that it was a young man named Zhang Sheng, about whom there is a widely circulated tale. Zhang Sheng had a large estate and much livestock. His wife Guo Dingxiang was virtuous and beautiful. The two got along extremely well until he married a lazy and malicious concubine named Li Haitang. Before much time had passed Li succeeded in persuading Zhang to divorce his wife. Without her supervision, Zhang and Li squandered his wealth away within two years. Then the concubine walked out on him and remarried, while Zhang was reduced to begging. Weak from hunger, he passed out at the gate of a household one bitter cold winter day. A maid from the house discovered him and helped him into their kitchen where she gave him something to eat. On asking about the mistress, Zhang learned that not only was she a virtuous lady who took pleasure in helping others, especially the aged and the poor, but that she was also single. This aroused in him a feeling of deep admiration. When he saw the good lady coming toward him through the window, however, he realized that she was none other than his first wife Guo Dingxiang. Overcome with shame, he dared not face her. But where to hide? The hearth was the only possible place, so he crawled into the hearth and was burned to death. Discovering that her ex-husband had been burned to ashes, Guo was filled with feeling both of pity and sadness. She died not long after this tragedy occurred. When the Jade Emperor (King of the Heaven) learned of the story, he praised Zhang Sheng for his courage in admitting his mistakes and declared him to be the Kitchen God.

The worship of the Kitchen God has a very long history. The great Han Dynasty emperor Wu Di personally officiated at ceremonies the god's honor. China's Kitchen God functioned as a judge of the Family's morality, just as did the Fire God of the Hindu religion. Both of the Hindu Fire God and the Chinese Kitchen God mediated between the human world and that of the gods. The Kitchen God's manner of coming and going (the burning of his portrait sends him to the heaven) may have originated from the natural phenomena of lightning, which was superstitiously believed to be the means by which God sent fire to earth.

The Kitchen God was so deeply rooted in the heart of the Chinese people that both Taoism and Buddhism adopted the concept so as to facilitate their own expansion. Thus Taoist mythology evolved a Kitchen with a number of different titles fitting into their own rather complex pantheon. The Buddhists argued that their Kitchen God was fundamentally different from the Taoists in that theirs was a celesta being men who became a Buddhist monk during the Tang dynasty who then, after his death, was chosen to preside over the vegetarian diet of the monks. This is of course an obvious rationalization of the Buddhist accommodation to Chinese popular beliefs.

Words & Expressions

clamor /'klæmə (r)/ n. 喧闹，叫嚷；大声的要求
ascend/ə'send/ v. 攀登，登上；上升，升高，通往高处；升职，晋升；追溯，溯源
hearth /ha:θ/ n. 灶台；炉边；炉床；壁炉地面
shrine /ʃraɪn/ n. 圣地；神殿；神龛；圣祠
patron /'peɪtrən/ n. 有权势的保护人，庇护人
ordain/ɔ:'deɪn / vt. 任命某人为牧师；授某人以圣职；（上帝、法律等）命令；注定
malicious /mə'lɪʃəs/ adj. 恶意的，恶毒的，怀恨的
squander/'skwɒndə (r)/ vt. 浪费，挥霍；使分散；失去（机会）
pantheon /'pænθiən/ n. 万神殿
preside /prɪ'zaɪd/ v. 主持，担任主持；主管某地，掌管（局势）

1. *The Rites of Zhou*: 《周礼》是儒家经典，十三经之一，是西周时期的著名政治家、思想家、文学家、军事家周公旦所著。《周礼》在汉代最初名为《周官》，始见于

《史记·封禅书》。《周礼》中记载先秦时期社会政治、经济、文化、风俗、礼法诸制，多有史料可采，所涉及之内容极为丰富，无所不包，堪称中国文化史之宝库。

2. *Huai Nan Zi*：《淮南子》（又名《淮南鸿烈》《刘安子》）是西汉皇族淮南王刘安及其门客收集史料集体编写而成的一部哲学著作。《淮南子》在继承先秦道家思想的基础上，糅合了阴阳、墨家、法家和一部分儒家思想，但主要的宗旨属于道家。

3. The actual identity of the Kitchen God：历来对灶神的真实身份有多种解释，或许由于大多数饭都是老太太做的，人们起初认为灶神是位老太太。后来又认为是位年轻女子，最后逐渐统一起来，说灶神是一个名叫张生的年轻人。有许多关于张生的故事，传说张生家财万贯，牲畜无数，妻子郭氏美丽贤惠，夫妻恩爱幸福。后来张生又纳李氏为妾，李氏好吃懒做，阴险毒辣，没过多日，李氏便教唆张生休了正妻郭氏。没了郭氏的经营，张生和李氏两年便把财产挥霍一空。之后李氏出走改嫁，而张生开始讨饭。他饥饿难耐，有个冬天晕倒在一妇人家的大门口，妇人出来见了把他扶进厨房，给了他一些吃的。张生问起女主人，得知这家女主人乐善好施，爱帮助老人和穷人，却是独居。张生顿生钦佩之情，透过窗户他看见女主人朝他走来，突然，他认出女主人正是他的前妻郭氏。张生深感羞愧，无颜面对妻子，他想了想，只有藏在灶里，于是他爬进灶里被火烧死了。看见丈夫被烧死，郭氏揪心地痛，没过多久便伤心而死。玉皇大帝闻知，念张生肯于悔过，又是在灶里被烧死的，便封他为灶神。

Reading Comprehension

Ⅰ. **Each piece of the following information is given in one of the paragraphs in the passage. Identify the paragraph from which the information is derived and put the corresponding number in the space provided.**

(　　) 1. In ancient China the Kitchen God commanded very high prestige among the people.

(　　) 2. Each household had s shrine for the Kitchen God in a corner on the back wall behind the hearth.

(　　) 3. The worship of the Kitchen God dates back over 2000 years.

(　　) 4. China's Kitchen God functioned as a judge of the Family s morality, just as did the Fire God of the Hindu religion.

(　　) 5. The Kitchen God was so deeply rooted in the heart of the Chinese people that both Taoism and Buddhism adopted the concept so as to facilitate their own expansion.

Ⅱ. **Decide whether the statements are true (T) or false (F) according to the passage.**

(　　) 1. Amidst the clamor of preparations for the Lunar New Year, time until the 23rd day of the 12th lunar month, when the time came to make offerings to the Kitchen God (Zaowangye).

(　　) 2. When a special god of fire appeared in the Chinese pantheon, he was worshipped as a family god and the protector of the hearth.

(　　) 3. Ancient people used to burn candles before his shrine only on the festival to respect the Kitchen God.

(　　) 4. The actual identity of the Kitchen God has been the subject of numerous interpretations over the course of time.

(　　) 5. The Kitchen God's manner of coming and going may have originated from the natural phenomena of lightning, which was superstitiously believed to be the means by which God sent fire to earth.

III. Discuss the following questions.
1. What was the shrine for the Kitchen God?
2. What was the actual identity of the Kitchen God?

第三章 农耕节日

Chapter 3　Farming Festivals

清明节
Qingming Festival

Qingming is a special festival in the sense that it does not come on a fixed day. It comes in the 3rd lunar month-around 5th of April of Gregorian calendar. Originally it was not a festival, but one of the seasonal divisions of the lunar year.

The lunar year is divided into 24 equal periods to mark the change of weather and farming situations. Around Qingming the weather gets mild with the rainy season setting in. It is the plowing and sowing season.

Qingming as a festival and a division of the year is full of poetic activities.

Of the ancient poems about Qingming, the one by the Tang of the poet Du Mu is a household poem and has come down to the present day. It goes roughly like this: Qingming's day is a rainy day, and people with a broken heart are back and forth on the way. May I ask where I can find a wine shop? The shepherd kid, pointing afar, says there you can find the best. This is a vivid description of the mood you felt on Qingming Festival.

The Song artist Zhang Zeduan's painting *Riverside Scene at Qingming Festival* (《清明上河图》) is a masterpiece of art. It describes what happens on both banks of the Bian River on the suburbs of the North Song capital on Qingming Festival. There is a long procession of people from all walks of life bustling along, some taking carriages, others sitting in sedans, on their way to the suburbs for spring outings. When you look at the picture you feel like part of it.

Qingming was the most important festival of the year in ancient times and spring outing was the most important part of the Qingming custom, therefore, it was the major theme for poetry and paintings. Yes, indeed, when willow trees turn green and peaches turn red and, sometimes, fine rains drizzle along with gentle breezes and you go outing in search of the spring mood, you are sure to feel refreshed in mind and heart.

Willow planting was another practice of the Qingming custom. The ancient Chinese enjoyed planting willows when Qingming came. They planted willows by the river and by the well. To plant willows by the well had, by the homophonic effect, the significance of living a well-arranged life.

During Qingming you would find people wearing willow on the heads, a kind of headwear woven with willow twigs, which they believed could exorcize evils. There were such sayings about wearing willow among the folks as "with a willow headwear on your head you will stay young, if not, you will get old" and "if you do not wear willow, you will become a dog". Though they do not sound very polite, they tell us in ancient times people cherished affectionate feelings for willow. Somewhere down the road in history, people quit wearing willow and began planting it and it is a very common custom today.

Literally Qingming means "clear" and "bright" with reference to the weather. When the weather was clear and sunny and the air fresh it was time for physical exercises. And also, on the Cold Food Festival the folks ate lots of delicious but cold food and they needed exercises to warm up and expel the cold air from the body. So in the poems and paintings about Qingming you see people playing ball games, tug-of-war, flying kites and on the swing.

Ball game was the most favorite game during Cold Food and Qingming Festival. During Tang Dynasty poems were composed to describe ball games that were similar to today's football. It was played not only by men, but also by women. It is now a common belief that football originated in China but it is not known to many people that football game was an important custom on Qingming Festival.

There was another ball game played on Qingming Festival that was played with the players riding horses like today's polo. It was also a game through which army officers were selected. In Tang and Song Dynasty polo was such a popular game as to attract the Emperor, not to mention the ordinary soldiers. On Qingming Festival the Emperor would grant a colored leather ball to his ministers and let them play with it in the field surrounded by a large audience watching while eating snacks. The Tang poet Zhang Ji says in his poem: "The imperial chef is dishing out the cold snacks along the hallway while the horses are galloping after the ball in front of the Hall." The great Tang writer and poet Han Yu also wrote about the polo game in his collected essays, asking his chief not to play the game because it was too dangerous. Though his chief did not take his advice, through his writings we know it was a violent as well as a popular game.

The earliest tug-of-war as a game was played in the State of Chu during the Spring and Autumn period. In warfare fought on waters, ropes made with leather and consolidated with bamboo were used to catch the enemy's battleships and then pull them over. The rope was called "towing hook" at that time. Later it became a game and a military exercise. And then it was adopted by the folks and became a popular game. During Tang Dynasty the game was known as "tug-of-war" and played on Qingming Festival. The rope was made of hemp, about 40~50 feet long, with several hundred short ropes attached to both ends. The players for both sides could add up to one thousand. Each side would have the end loops of the short ropes around their waists and dragged in opposite directions. A flag was stood in the middle and the side dragged over the flag was the loser. When the game was going on you could hear of deafening drums beating and cheerleaders shouting. An exciting sight. Tug-of war was also a popular game in the Tang court and Emperor Xuanzong himself was fond of it. He wrote a poem to encourage his soldiers and generals. He says in the poem if you want to cultivate your willpower like a hero's, go and play a lot of the game of win or lose.

The more poetic games were kite flying and swinging. When you watched kites flying in the sky in a sunny spring day or a swing going back and forth after a drizzling rain, you felt intoxicated.

It is said that during the Spring and Autumn period the famous legendary carpenter Lu Ban once made an eagle kite wood. He flew it up into the sky and it remained and floated adrift there for several dozen days running. It was perhaps the mother of all kites. After paper was invented, there were kites made of paper and they were called zhi yuan-paper eagle. And then a bamboo whistle was fixed to the head of the eagle. When it flew against the wind the sound it made was like the melody of the ancient Chinese instrument guzheng and that was why kite was called fengzheng (feng—wind, zheng—musical instrument). One of the Tang poem says "the blue sky is echoed with the strings on a silent night: the wind drifting around with different pitches". It describes the pleasant sounds made by the whistle attached to the kite.

Riding on the swing was a mimic of life of the primitive people. In those days people looking for food in the forest would catch hold of tree branches or rattan, swinging back and forth. A northern tribe called Shanrong was the first to adopt it as an entertainment. Duke Huan of the Qi State during the Spring and Autumn period after conquering Shanrong brought the game to Zhongyuan-central China. The game was officially named Qiuqian swinging in Han Dynasty. Mostly it was a game for girls. They tied the ends of a rope to trees and sat on the knot of the rope trying to swing as high as possible, with their colorful dresses trailing up and down like an angel flying. It was described in poems by Tang and Song poets-a proof of its popularity in ancient times.

Today, qiuqian and swing kites are played in many parts of the country and all the year round. They have become daily entertainments of the ordinary people. The famous International Kites Festival in Weifang, Shandong Province, is scheduled in April, maintaining much of the Qingming custom.

Words & Expressions

bustle /'bʌs(ə)l/ *v.* 四下忙碌；使（人沿某方向）匆忙地走；繁忙
drizzle /'drɪz(ə)l/ *vt.* （毛毛雨似地）洒；（在食物上）浇（液态调料）；*vi.* 下毛毛雨
homophonic /ˌhɒməˈfɒnɪk/ *adj.* 齐唱的

twig /twɪg/ *n.* 小枝，嫩枝
exorcize /ˈeksɔːsaɪz/ *vt.* 除怪，驱邪
affectionate /əˈfekʃənət/ *adj.* 表达爱意的，深情的
gallop /ˈgæləp/ *v.* （马）飞跑，飞奔；骑马奔驰，使（马）疾驰
consolidate /kənˈsɒlɪdeɪt/ *v.* 使巩固，使加强；合并，统一
mimic /ˈmɪmɪk/ *adj.* 模仿的，模拟的；假装的
primitive /ˈprɪmətɪv/ *adj.* 原始的，远古的
rattan /ræˈtæn; ˈrætæn/ *n.* 藤；藤杖，藤条

Notes

1. Zhang Zeduan's painting *Riverside Scene at Qingming Festival*: 《清明上河图》，为北宋风俗画，北宋画家张择端仅见的存世精品。清明上河图宽24.8厘米、长528.7厘米，绢本设色。作品以长卷形式，采用散点透视构图法，生动记录了中国12世纪北宋都城东京（又称汴京，今河南开封）的城市面貌和当时社会各阶层人民的生活状况，是北宋时期都城东京当年繁荣的见证，也是北宋城市经济情况的写照。

2. The Tang poet Zhang Ji says in his poem "The imperial chef is dishing out the cold snacks along the hallway while the horses are galloping after the ball in front of the Hall." 唐代诗人张籍"廊下御厨分冷食，殿前香骑逐飞球"。

3. Emperor Xuanzong himself was fond of it. He wrote a poem to encourage his soldiers and generals. 唐玄宗李隆基《观拔河俗戏》：壮徒恒贾勇，拔拒抵长河。欲练英雄志，须明胜负多。噪齐山岌嶪，气作水腾波。预期年岁稔，先此乐时和。

Reading Comprehension

I. Each piece of the following information is given in one of the paragraphs in the passage. Identify the paragraph from which the information is derived and put the corresponding number in the space provided.

(　　) 1. The Song artist Zhang Zeduan's painting *Riverside Scene at Qingming Festival* is a masterpiece of art.

(　　) 2. Qingming was the most important festival of the year in ancient times and spring outing was the most important part of the Qingming custom.

(　　) 3. During Qingming you would find people wearing willow on the heads, a kind of headwear woven with willow twigs, which they believed could exorcize evils.

(　　) 4. Ball game was the most favorite game during Cold Food and Qingming Festival.

(　　) 5. The more poetic games were kite flying and swinging.

II. Decide whether the statements are true (T) or false (F) according to the passage.

(　　) 1. It comes in the 3rd lunar month-around 4th of April of Gregorian calendar.

( ) 2. Around Qingming the weather gets mild with the rainy season setting in.

( ) 3. The earliest tug-of-war as a game was played in the State of Chu during Tang Dynasty.

( ) 4. It is said that during the Spring and Autumn period the famous legendary carpenter Lu Ban once made an eagle kite wood.

( ) 5. The game was officially named Qiuqian swinging in Han Dynasty.

Language Focus

III. Complete the sentences with the correct form of the words in the table.

consolidate	Originally	adrift	trail	originate
bustle	drizzle	homophonic	affectionate	primitive

1. _____ it was not a festival, but one of the seasonal divisions of the lunar year.

2. There is a long procession of people from all walks of life _____ along, some taking carriages, others sitting in sedans, on the their way to the suburbs for spring outings.

3. When willow trees turn green and peaches turn red and, sometimes, fine rains _____ along with gentle breezes.

4. To plant willows by the well had, by the _____ effect, the significance of living a well-arranged life.

5. Though they do not sound very polite, they tell us in ancient times people cherished _____ feelings for willow.

6. It is now a common belief that football _____ in China but it is not known to many people that football game was an important custom on Qingming Festival.

7. In warfare fought on waters, ropes made with leather and _____ with bamboo were used to catch the enemy's battleships and then pull them over.

8. He flew it up into the sky and it remained and floated _____ there for several dozen days running.

9. Riding on the swing was a mimic of life of the _____ people. In those days people looking for food in the forest would catch hold of tree branches or rattan, swinging back and forth.

10. They tied the ends of a rope to trees and sat on the knot of the rope trying to swing as high as possible, with their colorful dresses _____ up and down like an angel flying.

IV. Match the sentences in Section A with the English translation in Section B.

Section A

1. 清明那天，皇帝要把彩色鞠球赐给臣下，让他们在球场欢乐踢球。其余的人则围坐在球场外，边吃边看。

2. 荡秋千的习俗来源于原始社会时期人类的生活劳作。

3. 在井边插柳条，还有盼望今后日子能过得"井井有条"寓意。

4. 中国著名的潍坊国际风筝节，定在农历四月举行，似乎还保留了清明节放风筝的传统。

5. 阳春三月，桃红柳绿，和风拂面，细雨纷飞。

Section B

1. When willow trees turn green and peaches turn red and, sometimes, fine rains drizzle along with gentle breezes.

2. To plant willows by the well had, by the homophonic effect, the significance of living a well-arranged life.

3. On Qingming Festival the Emperor would grant a colored leather ball to his ministers and let them play with it in the field surrounded by a large audience watching while eating snacks.

4. Riding on the swing was a mimic of life of the primitive people.

5. The famous International Kites Festival in Weifang, Shandong Province, is scheduled in April, maintaining much of the Qingming custom.

V. Translate the paragraph into Chinese.

Literally Qingming means "clear" and "bright" with reference to the weather. When the weather was clear and sunny and the air fresh it was time for physical exercises. And also, on the Cold Food Festival the folks ate lots of delicious but cold food and they needed exercises to warm up and expel the cold air from the body. So in the poems and paintings about Qingming you see people playing ball games, tug-of-war, flying kites and on the swing.

_____

_____

_____

Development

VI. Discuss the following questions.

1. What activities do Chinese carry out on Qingming Festival?

2. Why, of the 24 solar terms, is Qingming celebrated as a festival?

Text B 端午节 Dragon Boat Festival

In Chinese language and culture, duanwu refers to 5th of 5th lunar month and this festival is also called "double fifth festival", but its English translation is Dragon Boat

Festival.

In ancient times duanwu was a festival to worship the Dragon. The people in the south-east parts of China believed they were the descendants of the dragon and the Dragon was their totem. On 5th of 5th lunar month they would hold grand sacrificial ceremonies. They rowed dragon boats throwing offerings into the water as they rowed along. Traditionally, they held dragon boat races and ate zongzi (a kind of dumpling wrapped in bamboo or reed leaves). The patriotic poet Qu Yuan of the State of Chu during the Warring States period (475 BC—221 BC) felt that he was incapable of saving his state from falling and committed suicide by drowning in water on 5th of 5th lunar month. People loved Qu Yuan and made this day a festival to the memory of the great poet.

As for the origin of Dragon Boat Festival there have been some arguments, but the one accepted by the people in general is related with Qu Yuan and so are the duanwu customs that have come down through history.

When Qu Yuan threw himself into the river, people who had learned of it rushed their boats over, trying to save him, but his body was engulfed by the waves on the vast expanse the river and he was nowhere to be found. The dragon boat races held on Dragon Boat Festival today demonstrate how the flustered boatmen in their desperate efforts tried to save him from being drowned.

Dragon boat race is a magnificent ceremony held on duanwu. The Miluo River is a tributary of Xiangjiang River in the northeast of Hunan Province. Every year the Dragon boat races held on this river attract hundreds of thousands of people to watch. On the morning of duanwu, the local people, dressed in their best clothes, will carry the movable dragon heads and swarm to Qu Yuan Temple for the ritual of a sacrifice to him and then stand along the river while dragon boats are pushed into the river one by one. The boats are hollowed out of single tree trunks of 25 or so meters in length and one meter in diameter. When the race is about to begin, the dragon head is fixed to the boat, projected high over the water. The head is delicately carved and the mouth can open and close with the tongue moving up and down inside. The head has a horn on each side with auspicious words written on them like "good weather brings good crops" etc. The dragon boats are in different colors black, yellow and white with the colors of the flag, oars and boatmen's clothes to match.

There are 36 oarsmen in 18 pairs in a racing-boat's crew. Each oarsman wears a bamboo hat with ornaments like birds and flowers, a Chinese-style shirt, a pair of trousers and a silk belt tied around the lower part of the shirt, rowing with a six-foot oar and the oarsmen are directed by the director standing at the head of the boat. Usually the director is an elderly person in a long gown with a short vest over it. He has by his side a boy wearing a girl's cloth and make-up, beating a gong.

When a firecracker goes off the race begins. The boats set off like arrows shot off the bows. Audiences on both banks burst into thunder-like applauses with firecrackers adding to the atmosphere. The folks, carrying chickens, ducks and rice wine and waving colorful silk strips in their hands, follow the boats and cheer them up. Girls, keeping in step with the rhythm of the racing boats, will sing dragon boat folk songs. It is a riot of festive excitement.

While boat racing is a popular game in south China that is rich in water resources, zongzi is a delicacy almost in every corner of the country. This custom is also related with Qu Yuan.

When the local people heard that Qu Yuan had drowned in the river, they tried to save him but failed. However, they believed that they could keep Qu Yuan's body intact by throwing food into the water to lure fish and tortoises away from Qu Yuan's body. To begin with, they filled bamboo tubes with rice and later they wrapped glutinous rice with moxa's leaves and fed it to fish and tortoises in the river. And this practice became a custom typical of duanwu and it has come down to the present day. This food glutinous rice wrapped with plants' leaves-is what we call zongzi today.

There is another version of the story about zongzi. It says that the bamboo tubes filled with glutinous rice were meant as an offering to Qu Yuan but unfortunately the zongzi thrown into the river were all taken by flood dragons. Later people discovered that glutinous rice wrapped with moxa's leaves and tied with colorful silk threads could scare the flood dragons away with its color and smell. This offering was called zongzi.

Some other people said that the first person who made this type of zongzi was a man named Ou Hui from Changsha—today's Hunan capital city. One night Ou Hui had a dream in which Qu Yuan passed to him this method of making zongzi. Whatever the stories say about zongzi, they manifest the love people cherish for Qu Yuan.

Originally zongzi was called jiaoshu. It was called Jiao because of its sharp projections and shu means the glutinous rice as its content. As its sharp projections resemble the veins of palm (pronounced zonglu in Chinese) leaves, the name of zongzi is a homophonic application of the first character of zonglus (palm tree) name. Since Tang and Song Dynasty zongzi has developed a great variety of contents. There is zongzi with rice only and zongzi with other ingredients, some sweet and others salty. For the sweet zongzi, the content of glutinous rice is mixed with sweetened bean paste, dates, lotus seeds, walnut, etc. and for the salty zongzi you can find pork, ham, egg, etc. in glutinous rice. The wrapper is different, though. Bamboo leaves and reeds leaves are used for their more pleasant flavor. Northerners prefer sweet triangle zongzi and southerners prefer square salty ones. The most famous zongzi are produced in Beijing, Suzhou, Guangdong, Zhejiang and Taiwan.

During Dragon Boat Festival people also drank realgar wine carried fragrant bags and hung sweet flags and moxa at the gate. Ancient Chinese believed that realgar was good to the health and, on Dragon Boat Festival, they sprayed realgar water indoors and outdoors. But modern science shows that realgar is a harmful mineral, so the custom has been discarded. Fragrant bags are made of silk and filled with medical herbs and perfumes to keep off poisonous insects. Sweet flags and moxa are also medical herbs with volatile juice that can clean the air and kill bacteria. Realgar, sweet flags and moxa are related with Qu Yuan because they were the things people threw into the water to keep fish, tortoise and flood dragons away from Qu Yuan's body.

Words & Expressions

descendant /dɪˈsendənt/ n. 后裔，子孙
totem /ˈtəʊtəm/ n. 图腾；崇拜物
sacrificial /ˌsækrɪˈfɪʃl/ adj. 牺牲的，献祭的
engulf /ɪnˈɡʌlf/ v. 吞没，淹没；使陷入（某种思绪或情绪）
fluster /ˈflʌstə(r)/ v.（使）忙乱，紧张；（使）心烦意乱
tributary /ˈtrɪbjətri/ n.（大河或湖泊的）支流
hollow /ˈhɒləʊ/ v. 使凹陷，使下陷；挖洞（成某物）；形成空洞
oar /ɔː(r)/ n. 橹，桨；桨手
ornament /ˈɔːnəmənt/ n. 装饰品
gong /ɡɒŋ/ n. 锣
glutinous /ˈɡluːtənəs/ adj. 黏的，胶质的
moxa /ˈmɒksə/ n. 艾
realgar /rɪˈælɡə(r)/ n. 雄黄
discard /dɪsˈkɑːd/ v. 扔掉，弃置
volatile /ˈvɒlətaɪl/ adj.（液体或固体）易挥发的，易气化的

Notes

1. Miluo River: 汨罗江是主要流经湖南平江县及湘阴东部（今县级汨罗市），发源于江西修水黄龙山梨树塬的南洞庭湖滨湖区最大河流。诗人屈原曾于公元前 278 年农历五月初五投汨罗江自杀，著名诗人余光中曾来到汨罗江畔祭祀屈原，诗中写道："蓝墨水的上游是汨罗江。"他用"蓝墨水"指代当代中华文脉，"汨罗江"则代指屈原。

2. Ou Hui from Changsha—today's Hunan capital city: 汉代长沙人欧回，他在梦中遇到了屈原，屈原传授了他这种方法。其实包粽子是为了喂饱鱼还是吓退蛟龙的传说本身并不重要，重要的是这一习俗，反映出人们对屈原的爱戴与怀念。

3. zongzi: 粽子最早叫"角黍"。"角"是说它的形状有棱有角，"黍"是指它用黍米做成。因为它的角尖尖的，像是棕榈叶心，后来人们就用了一个谐音的"粽"字来称呼它。

Reading Comprehension

I. **Each piece of the following information is given in one of the paragraphs in the passage. Identify the paragraph from which the information is derived and put the corresponding number in the space provided.**

(　　) 1. The patriotic poet Qu Yuan felt that he was incapable of saving his state from falling and committed suicide by drowning in water on 5th of 5th lunar month.

(　　) 2. Dragon boat race is a magnificent ceremony held on duanwu.

(　　) 3. While boat racing is a popular game in south China that is rich in water resources.

(　　) 4. Since Tang and Song Dynasties zongzi has developed a great variety of contents.

(　　) 5. During Dragon Boat Festival people also drank realgar wine carried fragrant bags and hung sweet flags and moxa at the gate.

II. Decide whether the statements are true (T) or false (F) according to the passage.

(　　) 1. In ancient times duanwu was a festival to worship the Dragon and Phenix.

(　　) 2. People loved Qu Yuan and made this day a festival to the memory of the great poet.

(　　) 3. The origin of Dragon Boat Festival accepted by the people in general is related with Qu Yuan and so are the Duan Wu customs that have come down through history.

(　　) 4. When the race is about to begin, the dragon tail is fixed to the boat, projected high over the water.

(　　) 5. The director has by his side a girl wearing a boy's cloth, beating a gong.

Development

III. Discuss the following questions.

1. Why did people hold dragon boat race and eat zongzi?
2. What do you know about zongzi?

Text C 丰收节 Chinese Farmers' Harvest Festival

Initiated in 2018, the Chinese Farmers' Harvest Festival coincides with the Autumn Equinox on lunar Chinese calendar each year. Falling on September 23rd this year, it is the first national festival held specifically for farmers, featuring a variety of activities, such as live-stream promotion, cultural performances, fairs, farming experiences communications and more.

This year marks the fourth Chinese Farmers' Harvest Festival, the first to be held since the law on the promotion of rural vitalization was adopted by the national legislature in April. So, why did the nation want to launch a festival especially for farmers and make it a lawful event? Peasants, the largest proportion of the Chinese population, have made great contributions to national development. Han Changfu, the Minister of Agriculture and Rural Affairs, said in 2018 before the launch of the festival that it would greatly encourage the passion and creativity of hundreds of millions of farmers and enhance their sense of happiness.

Can we expect a bumper harvest under the influence of natural disasters? Follow CGTN (China Global Television Network) to different locations and explore the festival.

The Chinese Farmers' Harvest Festival this year will hold major events along the Yangtze River Economic Belt on September 23rd to celebrate the harvest, promote culture and vitalize rural areas amid the centenary of the Communist Party of China, the Ministry of Agriculture and Rural Affairs said on Wednesday.

Three major events of the festival will be held in Jiaxing, Zhejiang Province; Changsha, capital of Hunan Province; and Deyang, Sichuan Province, with 11 cities and provinces in the region taking part, Vice-Minister Ma Youxiang said. Farmers will celebrate and perform in 1652 villages of ethnic groups, praising their agricultural achievements while enjoying the events held especially for them. "Nearly a hundred activities, such as cultural research, product promotion, folk festivals and farmers' competitions will be organized," Ma said. Focusing on farmers' happiness and needs, this year's festival will promote the launch of a series of policies and measures that benefit them, as well as the civil law and rural vitalization. It will also feature a free clinic week. "The farmers' sense of achievement, happiness and security are the most important criteria for evaluating the success of the harvest festival," Ma said. This year's festival is a celebration for farmers and also a grand event for urban residents. Modern agricultural exhibitions and rural food appreciation events are expected to draw many visitors. "The lively and popular activities will stimulate the passions of the farmers and residents," he said. The festival will continue to integrate farming culture and display cultural resources with local and ethnic characteristics. It will feature cultural activities such as farmers' concerts, rural photography, calligraphy and painting. "It will have both rustic flavor and cultural charm," Ma said. The festival aims to celebrate the bumper harvest while increasing farmers' incomes. The ministry will launch a "golden autumn consumption season" with other departments to promote urban and rural consumption.

A gala in the Beijing Expo park raised the curtain on activities celebrating the Chinese Farmers' Harvest Festival in northwestern Beijing's Yanqing District on September 22nd. At the gala, officials from Yanqing revealed various activities for the festival, such as sightseeing, food tasting and rural experience. Six boutique tourist routes were also set for the upcoming National Day holiday which lasts from Oct. 1st~7th, whereby tourists could enjoy the fun of fruit and vegetable picking, vanilla-themed travel, winter Olympic tour, and the Great Wall culture and leisure tour. In addition to the gala show, farmers in Yanqing displayed their agricultural products featuring organic milk, organic vegetables, volatile oil and chrysanthemum tea in the expo park, the venue of the 2019 Beijing International Horticultural Exhibition.

Farmers in suburban Songjiang District showed and shared their crops, livestock as well as the joy of harvest as they celebrated the fourth Chinese Farmers' Harvest Festival on Thursday. Exhibitions, live broadcast and a farmer market featuring seasonal fruits, vegetables, rice, and other agricultural products as well as historical materials, were held at Songjiang's Yun Jian Granary Cultural and Creative Park to celebrate the symbiotic relationship between farms and the natural world. A large number of precious historical materials and objects showing the historical evolution of Songjiang's agricultural development over the past century were displayed at the exhibition. Farmers from different kinds of cooperatives presented and sold their products at the bazaar. Songjiang Rice, a nationally known rice variety, was a favorite. The history of rice breeding in Songjiang dates back to the Song Dynasty, according to historical records.

The action highlights the government's emphasis on agriculture and rural areas and its people, drawing the whole society's attention to Chinese farmers, who diligently work to prop up the country's social and economic development. The government has also expressed its determination to see a thriving agricultural industry, beautiful countryside and well-off farmers.

The festival will surely be accompanied by certain rituals which are especially important to China, an agricultural giant with thousands of years of history. A whole year's tillage of the land brings big harvests, filling farmers with joy.

This festival will not only celebrate harvests but it will also be a reminder that more attention needs to be paid to agriculture and farmers, as well as traditional culture. The decision to set up this festival is not only for nostalgia or revelry, but to better embrace the future.

Words & Expressions

coincide /ˌkəʊɪnˈsaɪd/ v. 巧合，同时发生；一致，相符；相交，重叠
vitalization /ˌvaɪtlaɪˈzeɪʃən/ n. 振兴
legislature /ˈledʒɪslətʃə(r)/ n. 立法机关；立法机构
centenary /senˈtiːnəri/ n. 一百周年（纪念）
rustic /ˈrʌstɪk/ adj. 乡村的；纯朴的
calligraphy /kəˈlɪɡrəfi/ n. 书法，书法艺术
boutique /buːˈtiːk/ adj. 精品的
chrysanthemum /krɪˈzænθəməm; krɪˈsænθəməm/ n. 菊花
symbiotic /ˌsɪmbaɪˈɒtɪk/ adj. 共生的；共栖的
bazaar /bəˈzɑː(r)/ n. 集市；市场
tillage /ˈtɪlɪdʒ/ n. 耕作，耕种
nostalgia /nɒˈstældʒə/ n. 怀旧，念旧
revelry /ˈrevlri/ n. 狂欢；欢宴

Notes

Chinese Farmers' Harvest Festival: 中国农民丰收节，是第一个在国家层面专门为农民设立的节日，于2018年设立，节日时间为每年秋分。举办中国农民丰收节可以展示农村改革发展的巨大成就，同时，也展现了中国自古以来以农为本的传统。2021

年，四川德阳、湖南长沙、浙江嘉兴分别代表长江上中下游，承担中国农民丰收节组织指导委员会层面的三个主场活动。

Reading Comprehension

I. **Each piece of the following information is given in one of the paragraphs in the passage. Identify the paragraph from which the information is derived and put the corresponding number in the space provided.**

(　　) 1. Falling on September 23rd this year, it is the first National Festival held specifically for farmers, featuring a variety of activities, such as live-stream promotion, cultural performances, fairs, farming experiences communications and more.

(　　) 2. Nearly a hundred activities, such as cultural research, product promotion, folk festivals and farmers' competitions will be organized.

(　　) 3. Farmers in suburban Songjiang District showed and shared their crops, livestock as well as the joy of harvest as they celebrated the fourth Chinese Farmers' Harvest Festival on Thursday.

(　　) 4. The government has also expressed its determination to see a thriving agricultural industry, beautiful countryside and well-off farmers.

(　　) 5. This festival will not only celebrate harvests but it will also be a reminder that more attention needs to be paid to agriculture and farmers, as well as traditional culture.

II. **Decide whether the statements are true (T) or false (F) according to the passage.**

(　　) 1. Initiated in 2018, the Chinese Farmers' Harvest Festival coincides with the Spring Equinox on lunar Chinese calendar each year.

(　　) 2. This year's festival is a celebration exclusive for farmers, not for urban residents.

(　　) 3. In a gala in the Beijing Expo park, six boutique tourist routes were also set for the upcoming National Day holiday which lasts from Oct. 1st~7th, whereby tourists could enjoy the fun of fruit and vegetable picking, vanilla-themed travel, winter Olympic tour, and the Great Wall culture and leisure tour.

(　　) 4. Exhibitions, live broadcast and a farmer market featuring seasonal fruits, vegetables, rice, and other agricultural products as well as historical materials, were held to celebrate the symbiotic relationship between farms and the natural world.

(　　) 5. The history of rice breeding in Songjiang dates back to the Tang Dynasty, according to historical records.

Development

III. **Discuss the following questions.**

1. Please exemplify the celebration for Chinese Farmers' Harvest Festival.
2. What's the significance of Chinese Farmers' Harvest Festival?

第四章　农耕谚语

Chapter 4　Agricultural Proverbs

农耕谚语
About Agricultural Proverbs

China is an agricultural country with a vast territory, long history and brilliant culture. Chinese farmers have acquired rich experience in understanding and reforming nature throughout their daily life and work, which is expressed in agricultural proverbs and passed down orally from generation to generation. All nations and ethnic groups have proverbs widely used by their people. Proverbs are simple and pithy sayings that express truths based on common sense or experience of and insights into life. They are treasure of a culture and add metaphorical expressiveness to people's utterances and writings. Proverbs are usually concise but vivid, plain but philosophical and instructive, so they are hailed as poems of agricultural philosophy. Agricultural proverbs are an important component of Chinese agricultural civilization. Revealing natural laws conveying agricultural experience and spreading agricultural knowledge, they form an encyclopedia of agriculture and a sea of agricultural wisdom.

Farmers in ancient China created agricultural proverbs based on their experience in knowing, adapting themselves to and reforming the nature. These proverbs are passed down from generation to generation, polished and refined. Proverbs are the wit of one and the wisdom of many. Like two-part allegorical sayings (xiehouyu), antithetical couplets, the Tang and Song poetry, and traditional Chinese opera, proverbs are the brilliant inheritage of the ancient Chinese civilization.

Agricultural proverb is a kind of jargon very popular among peasants. In ancient times, the working people were illiterate. Their agricultural production experience mainly relied on the oral transmission and inheritance from father to his son, from brother to brother. Agricultural proverb is the main way to disseminate agricultural knowledge in Chinese history.

Similar as a technical instruction manual now, it has played an immeasurable role in production.

Agricultural proverbs are the crystallization of the experience accumulated by the working people in agricultural production practice, the collective creation of the people, and the precious agricultural and literary heritage of our people. Agricultural proverbs have the same origin with the Chinese agriculture, which even occurred before the written records. So the origin of agricultural proverbs can be traced back thousands of years. From the records of ancient books, we can see that there were poems similar to farm proverbs as early as slave society.

Agricultural proverbs summarize experience of agricultural practices and reveal the laws of agricultural production. Farmers learned when to do farming work, how to predict weather and how to improve agronomic techniques based on their experiences and observations. They knew how to make full use of the time, the land and physical conditions to improve production. Proverbs, such as "Make full use of every day in spring and every minute in summer, because time won't stop for farmers to catch up with" and "If wheat seedlings are covered by a thick snow quilt, farmers will sleep with steamed-bun-pillows the next year" reveal their knowledge about agriculture and nature.

These proverbs, with their simple dialectics, reflect farmers' scientific deep understanding of the relationship between man and nature. Such proverbs as "100% of harvest can only be ensured by 30% of cultivation and 70% of management" and "Humans plant trees today, and trees will repay them in the future" indicate Chinese farmers' reverence for nature. They tried to adapt to the time and the milieu. In order to feed and survive, the ancient Chinese farmers adopted intensive farming mode as well as intensive and fine management of their land.

Agricultural proverbs reflect Chinese people's deep understanding of the relationship between agriculture and daily life. Such proverb are "Rice is afraid of insects in autumn just as human beings are afraid of poverty when aged" and "A bucket of seeds are more preferred than a bucket of gold". These proverbs contain agricultural experience and life philosophy. They shed light on our life and social development.

Agricultural proverbs were created long time ago, but are still instructive today. General Secretary Xi Jinping's address at the 2013 Central Rural Work Conference in Beijing urged that government officials should know and learn by heart agricultural proverbs to better understand the basic knowledge of agriculture, as proverbs express commonly held ideas and beliefs in a vivid way.

China is now in a crucial stage of building a moderately prosperous society in an all-round way. Chinese people are now striving for the Chinese Dream of realizing the great rejuvenation of the country. The well-being of farmers is essential to a moderately prosperous society. The most arduous task of building a well-off society lies in the development of rural areas. The development of agriculture, rural areas and farmers pave the way for the realization of the Chinese Dream. It's significant to accelerate the agricultural modernization to keep up with the rapid development of industrialization, informatization, and urbanization. To speed up agricultural modernization, we should not only learn the cutting-edge technologies, but also learn from the wisdom of the ancient people by inheriting and promoting the traditional Chinese farming civilization. It is necessary to incorporate the modern mode of production and management with the traditional mode of intensive farming, thus agricultural modernization with Chinese characteristics.

The philosophy of harmony between human and nature reflected in Chinese agricultural proverbs is also enlightening to other nations and areas.

Words & Expressions

pithy/'pɪθi/*adj.* 精练的；简洁有力的
metaphorical/ˌmetə'fɒrɪkl/*adj.* 隐喻的，象征的
concise/kən'saɪs/*adj.* 简明的，简洁的
hail/heɪl/*v.* 赞扬，欢呼
encyclopedia/ɪnˌsaɪklə'piːdiə/*n.* 百科全书
allegorical/ˌælə'gɒrɪkl/*adj.* 讽喻的；寓言的，寓意的
antithetical/ˌæntɪ'θetɪkl/*adj.* 对立的，正相反的
couplet/'kʌplət/*n.* （尤为押韵等长的）对句，对联
jargon/'dʒɑːgən/*n.* 行话，黑话
disseminate/dɪ'semɪneɪt/*vt.* 宣传，传播；散布
agronomic/ˌægrə'nɒmɪk/*adj.* 农事的
dialectics/ˌdaɪə'lektɪks/*n.* 辩证法；辩证逻辑
reverence/'revərəns/*n.* 崇敬，尊严；敬礼
milieu/mɪl'jɜː/*n.* 环境

Notes

1. Make full use of every day in spring and every minute in summer, because time won't stop for farmers to catch up with. 春争日，夏争时，一年农事不宜迟。

2. If wheat seedlings are covered by a thick snow quilt, farmers will sleep with

steamed-bun-pillows the next year. 麦苗盖上雪花被，来年枕着馍馍睡。

3. 100% of harvest can only be ensured by 30% of cultivation and 70% of management. 三分种，七分管，十分收成才保险。

4. Humans plant trees today, and trees will repay them in the future. 今日人种树，他日树养人。

5. Rice is afraid of insects in autumn just as human beings are afraid of poverty when aged. 人怕老来穷，谷怕秋后虫。

6. A bucket of seeds are more preferred than a bucket of gold. 宁要一斗种，不要一斗金。

Reading Comprehension

I. Each piece of the following information is given in one of the paragraphs in the passage. Identify the paragraph from which the information is derived and put the corresponding number in the space provided.

(   ) 1. Proverbs are treasure of a culture and add metaphorical expressiveness to people's utterances and writings.

(   ) 2. Agricultural proverb is a kind of jargon very popular among peasants.

(   ) 3. Agricultural proverbs are the crystallization of the experience accumulated by the working people in agricultural production practice, the collective creation of the people, and the precious agricultural and literary heritage of our people.

(   ) 4. Agricultural proverbs were created long time ago, but are still instructive today.

(   ) 5. The philosophy of harmony between human and nature reflected in Chinese agricultural proverbs is also enlightening to other nations and areas.

II. Decide whether the statements are true (T) or false (F) according to the passage.

(   ) 1. Like two-part allegorical sayings (xiehouyu), antithetical couplets, the Tang and Song poetry, and traditional Chinese opera, proverbs are the brilliant inheritance of the ancient Chinese civilization.

(   ) 2. Their agricultural production experience mainly relied on the oral transmission and inheritance from father to his son, from brother to brother.

(   ) 3. From the records of ancient books, we can see that there were poems similar to farm proverbs as early as feudal society.

(   ) 4. Farmers learned when to do farming work, how to predict weather and how to improve agronomic techniques only based on their experiences.

(   ) 5. To speed up agricultural modernization, we should only learn the cutting-edge technologies, and ignore the wisdom of the ancient people.

Language Focus

III. Complete the sentences with the correct form of the words in the table.

philosopher	allegory	encyclopedia	urbanization	rejuvenation
metaphor	reverence	territory	disseminate	agronomy

1. China is an agricultural country with a vast _____, long history and brilliant culture.

2. They are treasure of a culture and add _____ expressiveness to people's utterances and writings.

3. Proverbs are usually concise but vivid, plain but _____ and instructive, so they are hailed as poems of agricultural philosophy.

4. Revealing natural laws conveying agricultural experience and spreading agricultural knowledge, they form an _____ of agriculture and a sea of agricultural wisdom.

5. Like two-part _____ sayings, antithetical couplets, the Tang and Song poetry, and traditional Chinese opera, proverbs are the brilliant inheritage of the ancient Chinese civilization.

6. Agricultural proverb is the main way to _____ agricultural knowledge in Chinese history.

7. Farmers learned when to do farming work, how to predict weather and how to improve _____ techniques based on their experiences and observations.

8. Proverbs indicate Chinese farmers' _____ for nature.

9. Chinese people are now striving for the Chinese Dream of realizing the great _____ of the country.

10. It's significant to accelerate the agricultural modernization to keep up with the rapid development of industrialization, informatization, and _____.

IV. Match the sentences in Section A with the English translation in Section B.

Section A

1. 农谚是劳动人民敬畏自然的体现，反映了顺应天时、善用地利的思想，古代农民集约经营、精细管理土地。

2. 农谚是对生产生活的深刻感悟，反映了中华民族的人生智慧。

3. 农谚是对农业实践的经验总结，揭示了农业生产的客观规律。

4. 小康不小康，关键看老乡；实现中国梦，基础在"三农"。全面建成小康社会，最艰巨、最繁重的任务在农村。

5. 农谚是对人与自然关系的科学把握，体现了朴素的辩证法思想。

Section B

1. Agricultural proverbs summarize experience of agricultural practices and reveal the laws of agricultural production.

2. These proverbs, with their simple dialectics, reflect farmers' scientific deep understanding of the relationship between man and nature.

3. Such proverbs indicate Chinese farmers' reverence for nature. They tried to adapt to the time and the milieu. In order to feed and survive, the ancient Chinese farmers adopted intensive farming mode as well as intensive and fine management of their land.

4. Agricultural proverbs reflect Chinese people's deep understanding of the relationship between agriculture and daily life.

5. The well-being of farmers is essential to a moderately prosperous society. The most arduous task of building a well-off society lies in the development of rural areas. The development of agriculture, rural areas and farmers pave the way for the realization of the Chinese Dream.

V. Translate the paragraph into Chinese.

China is an agricultural country with a vast territory, long history and brilliant culture. Chinese farmers have acquired rich experience in understanding and reforming nature throughout their daily life and work, which is expressed in agricultural proverbs and passed down orally from generation to generation. Proverbs are usually concise but vivid, plain but philosophical and instructive, so they are hailed as poems of agricultural philosophy. Agricultural proverbs are an important component of Chinese agricultural civilization. Revealing natural laws conveying agricultural experience and spreading agricultural knowledge, they form an encyclopedia of agriculture and a sea of agricultural wisdom.

_____
_____
_____
_____
_____

Development

VI. Discuss the following questions.

1. How did the ancient farmers observe the laws of agricultural production?
2. How did the ancient farmers balance the relationship between man and nature?

Text B 春、夏 Spring & Summer

Spring

立春一年端,种地早盘算。

Beginning of Spring is the start of a year when farmers should make farming schedules with no delay.

This solar term starts on February 3rd, 4th or 5th when the sun reaches the celestial longitude of 315°. After Beginning of Spring, the temperature is rising and farming activities are to start. People are supposed to make their farming plan promptly. However, at this time of the year, only southern China are in spring while most northern parts of the country remain in winter.

春争日，夏争时，一年农事不宜迟。

Make full use of every day in spring and every minute in summer, because time won't stop for farmers to catch up with.

Farming starts in spring. It is better to lose no time and start early. Summer is the time to harvest winter wheat and rapeseed as well as planting rice, cotton, corn, and soybean, etc. The weather in summer is subject to change, so it is necessary to make good use of every minute to harvest. This is also the case for crop sowing because crops yield higher if they are planted early in the season.

春打六九头，春耕早动手。

Beginning of Spring arrives on the first day of the sixth Nine-day period, and the spring farming must be started early.

In the Chinese lunar calendar, the days following the Winter Solstice are grouped into nine periods, which means a nine-day cycle, with each period numbered according to the sequence from first nine (yijiu) to ninth nine (jiujiu). Beginning of Spring in general comes on the last day of fifth nine (wujiu) or the first day of sixth nine (liujiu). It is the time to start the spring farming.

立春雨水到，早起晚睡觉。

Following Beginning of Spring comes Rain Water. Farmers get up early and go to bed late.

Rain Water comes immediately after Beginning of Spring. The temperature is rising and the sunlight hours and rainfall are increasing, which is conducive to crop growth. During Beginning of Spring and Rain Water, fields need watering and fertilizing in time to keep high moisture and nutrition level. They are also prepared a ploughed for the subsequent farming activities. Farmers have to labor from dawn to dusk to catch up with the tight schedule.

雨水有雨庄稼好，下多下少都是宝。

Rain in Rain Water is good to crop growth, be it light or heavy.

During Rain Water, overwintering crops begin to green up and spring crops are to be sown. They have a large demand for water.

不怕一冬旱，就怕正、二、三。

Winter drought is nothing to worry about, but spring drought is a big threat.

Crops do not need much water in winter when seedlings grow slowly, so a winter drought won't have much impact on crop growth. However, in spring, the first three months of the lunar calendar in particular, crops grow very quickly and have a larger demand for water. Should a drought hit at this time, crops would not grow fast and yields would be reduced.

惊蛰春雷响，农夫闲转忙。

Spring thunder during Waking of Insects calls on farmers to get busy.

Waking of Insects (March 5th, 6th or 7th) sees the start of the planting season when thunder can be heard now and then. The weather becomes warmer, the soil thaws, and hibernating animals wake up. Farmers get busy after a winter's rest.

惊蛰有雨并闪雷，麦积场中如土堆。

Rain with thunder in Waking of Insects promises piles of wheat on threshing grounds.

In northern China where spring drought occurs frequently, rain is very welcome by farmers. Rain supplements the soil moisture and is conducive to the growth of winter wheat. A good harvest is expected.

惊蛰麦返青，春分麦起身。

Wheat greens up in Waking of Insects and stands up in the Spring Equinox.

In northern China, when the temperature rises in spring, winter wheat starts to produce young leaves and tillers. Around Waking of Insects, the field will turn from yellow to green, which is called green-up. Then around the Spring Equinox, the wheat enters the jointing stage. Wheat seedlings rise from the ground and stand erect. This growth process is vividly depicted as "standing-up".

Summer

西瓜怕热雨，麦子怕热风。

Watermelon is afraid of hot rain while wheat hot wind.

Watermelons are setting fruit during Slight Fullness (May 20th, 21st or 22nd). Excessive heat will reduce the pollen viability. Rain will reduce the fertility of the stigma of both male and female flowers. Pollination, fertilization, and fructification will all be reduced. Wheat is at its milk-ripe stage during Slight Fullness. Dry and hot wind speeds up the ripening of wheat grains and leads to hollow seeds.

热熟谷，粒实鼓；热熟麦，糠一袋。

Heat brings plump grains for foxtail millet but hollow grains for wheat.

Foxtail millet likes hot weather in the ripening season. Heat helps it to produce plump grains. But if wheat is hit by dry hot wind during the ripening season, the grain filling will be insufficient, and the plants may produce a lot of hollow grains.

小满见三鲜。

Three kinds of fresh food are seen in Slight Fullness.

Various field crops, fruits, melons and vegetables ripen and are sold at the market during Slight Fullness. People buy these freshly picked foods and enjoy eating them. Different areas have their own groups of "three kinds of fresh food" according to the local customs. In the Yangtze River Delta Area, they are usually barley, oilseed and broad bean, but in the Yellow River and Huaihe River Area, they are wheat, garlic and silk cocoons.

夏至棉田草，如同毒蛇咬。

Weeds in the cotton fields during Summer Solstice are as poisonous as a serpent's bite.

This proverb compares weeds to serpents. During the Summer Solstice (June 21st or 22nd), weeds grow rapidly. Competing with crops for water and nutrients, they are detrimental to the crop growth. Therefore, it is necessary to till the fields to get rid of weeds.

小暑雨如银，大暑雨如金。

Rain in Slight Heat is as precious as silver while that in Great Heat is as precious as gold.

The moisture in the leaves evaporates quickly during Slight Heat and Great Heat (July 22nd, 23rd or 24th) when the temperature is high and the sun is strong. At this key time, crops need sufficient water to stay healthy. So, rain is very precious.

小暑天气热，棉花整枝不停数。

Do not stop pruning cotton plants during Slight Heat when the weather is very hot.

Cotton plants grow fast during Slight Heat (July 6th, 7th or 8th) when the weather becomes very hot. The plants need to be pruned continually by removing unnecessary branches, leaves and buds, as well as topping, to store nutrients for buding and boll opening.

小暑不算热，大暑正伏天。

The heat during Slight Heat is nothing compared with that of dog days during Great Heat.

Xiaoshu is not the hottest time of the year. The last few days of Great Heat, or the dog days, are the hottest.

大暑连天阴，遍地出黄金。

Cloudy days during Great Heat make fields filled with gold.

Dashu is the hottest time of the year. If the weather is cloudy continuously in Great Heat, crops won't suffer from extreme heat. A good harvest is expected in autumn.

Words & Expressions

  celestial /sə'lestiəl/ *adj.* 天空的，天上的；天国的，天堂的；精美绝伦的
  rapeseed /'reɪpsiːd/ *n.* 油菜籽
  fertilize /'fɜːtəlaɪz/ *vt.* 使受精；使肥沃
  thaws /θɔː/ *v.* （使）（冰雪）融化；（使）（冷冻食品）解冻；使（身体等）变得暖起来；变得友好，变得缓和
  hibernate /'haɪbəneɪt/ *v.* 冬眠；（人）（长期）蛰居，不活动
  thresh /θreʃ/ *v.* 打谷
  tiller /'tɪlə (r)/ *n.* （草）分蘖；（从基底部）出新芽

viability /ˌvaɪə'bɪləti/ n. 生存能力，发育能力
stigma /'stɪgmə/ n.（植物花朵的）柱头
pollination /ˌpɒlə'neɪʃn/ n. 授粉
fructification /ˌfrʌktɪfɪ'keɪʃən/ n. 果实；结实器官；结果实
plump /plʌmp/ adj. 饱满的
detrimental /ˌdetrɪ'ment(ə)l/ adj. 有害的，不利的
prune /pruːn/ v. 修剪，修整

Notes

1. Beginning of Spring is the start of a year when farmers should make farming schedules with no delay.

立春就是春季开始的意思，2 月 3、4 或 5 日太阳到达黄经 315°时，我国北方大多数地区仍处于冬季，真正进入春季的只有华南等地区。泛指立春以后，气温逐渐回升，春种春管等各项农事活动将陆续开始，提醒人们要及早谋划春季农业生产事宜。

2. Beginning of Spring arrives on the first day of the sixth Nine-day period, and the spring farming must be started early.

立春也称"打春"，从冬日起开始"数九"，每九天为一个"九"，一般到五九尾或六九开头的一天是立春。我国南方地区开始进入春耕备耕阶段。类似农谚有"春打六九头，七九、八九就使牛"等。

3. Wheat greens up in Waking of Insect and stands up in Spring Equinox.

春季气温逐步回升，北方地区冬小麦开始萌发新生叶片和分蘖，麦田景色在惊蛰节气前后由黄转绿，称为返青。此后小麦进入生物学拔节，麦苗由匍匐在地表转为直立，其生长过程形象地称为"起身"。

4. Three kinds of fresh food are seen in Slight Fullness.

泛指到了小满时节，各种各样的大田作物及瓜果蔬菜陆续成并收获上市，可供人们尝鲜，故也有"小满见三鲜"之说。但各所指"三新"或"三鲜"不同，江南地区多指大麦、油菜，黄淮地区多指小麦（仁）、大蒜、蚕茧。

Reading Comprehension

Ⅰ. Each piece of the following information is given in one of the paragraphs in the passage. Identify the paragraph from which the information is derived and put the corresponding number in the space provided.

(   ) 1. Beginning of Spring arrives on the first day of the sixth Nine-day period, and the spring farming must be started early.

(   ) 2. Crops do not need much water in winter when seedlings grow slowly, so a winter drought won't have much impact on crop growth.

(   ) 3. The moisture in the leaves evaporates quickly during Slight Heat and Great Heat (July 22nd, 23rd, or 24th) when the temperature is high and the sun is strong.

(　　) 4. The plants need to be pruned continually by removing unnecessary branches, leaves and buds, as well as topping, to store nutrients for buding and boll opening.

(　　) 5. Slight Heat is not the hottest time of the year. The last few days of Great Heat, or the dog days, are the hottest.

II. Decide whether the statements are true (T) or false (F) according to the passage.

(　　) 1. Farming starts in summer. It is better to lose no time and start early.

(　　) 2. The weather in summer is subject to change, so it is necessary to make good use of every minute to harvest.

(　　) 3. During Rain Water, crops don't have a large demand for water.

(　　) 4. Watermelons are setting fruit during Slight Fullness (May 20th, 21st or 22nd). Excessive heat will reduce the pollen viability.

(　　) 5. Different areas have their own groups of "three kinds of fresh food" according to the local customs. In the Yangtze River Delta Area, they are wheat, garlic and silk cocoons.

III. Discuss the following questions.

1. Why every day in spring and every minute in summer should be fully made use of?

2. In the Chinese lunar calendar, the days following Winter Solstice are grouped into nine periods. What do they mean?

秋、冬
Autumn & Winter

Autumn

立秋三场雨，遍地是黄金。

Three rainfalls in Beginning of Autumn produce a field of gold.

Beginning of Autumn (Aug. 7th, 8th or 9th) is the time when autumn crops, such as summer-sown corn, rice and beans, enjoy vigorous growth and fruiting. Rain is welcome as plenty of water is needed to ensure a good harvest.

立了秋，把头揪。

Top cotton during Beginning of Autumn.

Cotton is an indefinite inflorescence plant. It keeps budding and flowering if conditions permit, which consumes a large amount of nutrients. It takes about 70 to 80 days from budding to boll opening. To ensure the quality of cotton fiber, cotton plants need to be topped around

Beginning of Autumn so that cotton bolls will have enough nutrition to develop.

白露种高山，秋分种平川，寒露种沙滩。

Sow wheat in hillside fields during White Dew, on plains during Autumn Equinox and in sandy beaches during Cold Dew.

Winter wheat is sown at different times of the autumn according to the location of the fields. For fields on shady slopes in northern China, wheat is usually sown in White Dew, ahead of the usual schedule, because of the low temperature there. For fields on plains. it is sown during Autumn Equinox (Sept. 22nd, 23rd or 24th). However, for sandy fields on the beach, where the temperature is higher, it is sown during Cold Dew (Oct. 8th or 9th), later than on a the plain.

一场秋雨一场寒，秋分有雨丰来年。

Autumn rain brings chill with it, but rain during Autumn Equinox brings about a good harvest the next year.

Every rainfall in autumn makes the day chillier. Winter wheat is sown during or after Autumn Equinox Rainfall during this period increases the moisture content in the soil and is good for wheat.

秋分稻见黄，大风要提防。

Be cautious of gales during Autumn Equinox when rice turns yellow.

Rice is in the grain filling stage during Autumn Equinox. At this time of the year, blasts of cold air begin to invade. Rice is likely to produce unfilled grains when the temperature is too low. So, precautions must be taken in case that cold gales blow down the plants.

种麦砘子响，地里红薯长。

As the stone roller is creaking in wheat fields, sweet potatoes are growing rapidly.

A stone roller, or dunzi in Chinese, is a farming tool used to press the soil to make it solid when seeds are sown and covered by soil. This practice is beneficial for seed germination. The time when wheat is sown, sweet potatoes are in rapid growth.

寒露接霜降，秋收秋种忙。

Cold Dew is followed by Frost's Descent. Farmers are busy harvesting and planting.

Cold Dew is followed by Frost's Descent. During this period, the weather gets colder and colder. Therefore, it is urgent for farmers to harvest autumn crops and plant overwintering crops such as barley, heat oilseed rape, and garlic.

棉是秋后草，就怕霜来早。

Cotton is afraid of early autumn frost just as grass is.

Cotton has a long growth period. If it is planted too late, it won't be able to develop bolls fully when the temperature decreases quickly and frosts fall in autumn. Grass turns yellow and withers when frosts fall. So, what early autumn frosts are to cotton, they are the same to grass.

Winter

地不冻，犁不停。

Ploughs keep working until the soil freezes.

Deep ploughing promotes the soil conditions and is good for spring farming. So, it is necessary to plough the fields before the soil freezes deeply.

立冬下麦迟，小雪搞积肥。

Sowing wheat during Beginning of Winter is too late and compost should be applied during Slight Snow.

Sowing wheat during Beginning of Winter (Nov. 7th or 8th) is too late. Wheat seedlings will be too young to defend against cold damage. Therefore, compost should be applied to the fields during Slight Snow (Nov. 22nd or 23rd) to cover the seedlings protecting them from the cold and helping them to overwinter smoothly.

大雪小雪雪满天，来年准是丰收年。

Heavy snowfalls during Heavy Snow and Slight Snow promise a good harvest in the next year.

If it snows heavily during Slight Snow and Heavy Snow (Dec. 6th, 7th or 8th), snow will cover overwintering crops, such as winter wheat, like a thick quilt. It protects the seedlings from cold damage, kills insect pests, and keeps the moisture content in the soil. So a good harvest is expected in the next year.

大雪冬至雪花飘，兴修水利积肥料。

Construct water conservancy facilities and accumulate compost from Heavy Snow to Winter Solstice when snowflakes float in the sky.

The weather is too cold for farm work from Heavy Snow to Winter Solstice (Dec. 21st, 22nd or 23rd). Farmers have enough time to construct water conservancy facilities and produce compost.

麦苗盖上雪花被，来年枕着馍馍睡。

If wheat seedlings are covered by a thick snow quilt, farmers will sleep with *manton* pillows the next year.

Snow covers wheat seedlings like a thick quilt. It protects seedlings from cold damage if it's more than 30cm thick. Thick snow ensures a good harvest in the next year, so farmers will have much flour to make mantou (Chinese steamed buns).

大雪半融加一冰，来年病虫发生轻。

If partially melted snow freezes, crop diseases and pests will be reduced.

If the temperature falls when snow is melting during Heavy Snow, slush feeze. Bacteria and pests in the fields will also freeze to death. There will be less plant diseases and pests in the next year. But if a blast of cold air invades when snow has melted completely, water from melted snow will freeze. It is harmful to wheat.

大雪忙挖土，冬至压麦田。

Plough the fields during Heavy Snow while press wheat seedlings in Winter Solstice.

Ploughing the fields deeply before the soil freezes around Heavy Snow not only loosens the soil and improves its structure, but also helps to hold water. Pressing wheat seedlings with rollers when they grow vigorous around Winter Solstice promotes their cold resistance. It is better to press the seedlings in warm sunny afternoons. Seedlings grown in alkaline and sandy fields should not be pressed.

冬至过，地皮破。
Break the fields after Winter Solstice.

"Break the fields" means deep ploughing of the fields or the surface of the fields cracks by freezing weather in winter. Fields left vacant in winter should be thoroughly ploughed after Winter Solstice. By doing so, the soil is loosened and takes in rain or snow water easily. Exposing the deep layers of the soil to the sun also helps to kill bacteria and underground pests.

冬至大如年。
The festivity of Winter Solstice is comparable to that of the Spring Festival.

Winter Solstice marks the beginning of the coldest days of the year. Its arrival signals the coming of the Chinese lunar New Year. Chinese people celebrate it as joyfully as they celebrate the Spring Festival.

小寒三九天，把好防冻关。
Take precautions against coldness in Slight Cold which coincides with the third Nine-day period.

Slight Cold (Jan. 5th, 6th or 7th) indicates the coming of the coldest days of the year. In certain years, Slight Cold witnessed even colder weather than Great Cold (Jan 20th or 21st). Therefore, it is necessary to take precautions against cold damage to crops.

腊月三白，适宜麦菜。
Three snowfalls in the twelfth lunar month are a blessing for wheat and oilseed rape.

Frequent snowfalls in winter are beneficial to the growth of winter wheat and oilseed rape. Heavy Snow protects crops from extreme cold and helps to increase the soil moisture.

寒冬不寒，来年不丰。
No cold winter, no good harvest the next year.

A cold winter means a good harvest in the next year. Overwintering crops like wheat grow slowly and even stop growing when the weather is very cold in winter, so their parts above the ground will not be damaged by the cold. But in a warm winter crops grow fast, so their above ground parts joint earlier than usual and are easy to suffer from cold damage. Meanwhile, pests can survive warm winters, so crops are more likely to develop diseases.

Words & Expressions

inflorescence /ˌɪnflɔːˈres(ə)ns/ *n.* 花；花序；开花
gale /ɡeɪl/ *n.* 大风，狂风
germination /ˌdʒɜːmɪˈneɪʃn/ *n.* 发芽
barley /ˈbɑːli/ *n.* 大麦
boll /bəʊl/ *n.* [植] 圆荚

compost /ˈkɒmpɒst/ n. 堆肥；混合物
conservancy /kənˈsɜːvənsi/ n. 管理；保护；保存
quilt /kwɪlt/ n. 被子，被褥
slush /slʌʃ/ n. 烂泥；污水
alkaline /ˈælkəlaɪn/ adj. 碱性的；含碱的
bacteria /bækˈtɪəriə/ n. 细菌（bacterium 的复数）

Notes

1. "Three rainfalls" here does not mean rain three times, but abundant rain. The number three has special meaning in Chinese, Lao Tzu said in his *Dao De Jing* that "The Dao produced One; One produced Two; Two produced Three; Three produced All things" (James Legg's translation).

2. Break the fields after Winter Solstice.
过了冬至，冬季空闲的田块应该耕翻破垡，以便接纳冬季雨雪、熟化疏松土壤，少病虫越冬基数。另外，"地皮破"还有形容天气寒冷、地表受冻破裂的意思。

Reading Comprehension

I. **Each piece of the following information is given in one of the paragraphs in the passage. Identify the paragraph from which the information is derived and put the corresponding number in the space provided.**

(　　) 1. Rain is welcome as plenty of water is needed to ensure a good harvest.

(　　) 2. Every rainfall in autumn makes the day chillier.

(　　) 3. What early autumn frosts are to cotton, they are the same to grass.

(　　) 4. If it snows heavily during Slight Snow and Heavy Snow (Dec. 6th, 7th or 8th), snow will cover overwintering crops, such as winter wheat, like a thick quilt.

(　　) 5. Ploughing the fields deeply before the soil freezes around Heavy Snow not only loosens the soil and improves its structure, but also helps to hold water.

II. **Decide whether the statements are true (T) or false (F) according to the passage.**

(　　) 1. It takes about 60 to 90 days for cotton from budding to boll opening.

(　　) 2. Winter wheat is sown at different times of the autumn according to the location of the fields.

(　　) 3. If a blast of cold air invades when snow has melted completely, crop diseases and pests will be reduced.

(　　) 4. In certain years, Slight Cold witnessed even colder weather than Great Cold.

(　　) 5. A cold winter means that there will not be a good harvest in the next year.

Development

III. Discuss the following questions.

1. Why is cautious of gales during Autumn Equinox when rice turns yellow?
2. Why is the festivity of Winter Solstice comparable to that of the Spring Festival?

第五章 农耕艺术

Chapter 5 Farming Fine Arts

Text A 风筝 / Kites

China is home to one of the world's oldest civilizations. With a history of dynasties and city-states, this cultural hub of Asian invention flaunts a number of "firsts", including the invention of paper and kites. The earliest mention of a kite in ancient China dates back to the 5th century BC.

Kites also named "fengzheng" what is known in ancient as zhiyuan (paper kites) or muyuan (wooden kites), fall into two major groups—the southern group and the north group. In south China, kites are usually called yaozi (harrier) or banyao (wooden harrier), while in north China they are known as muyuan (wooden hawk), fengyan (wind hawk) or feiyuan (flying hawk). As a folk art, the Chinese kite is usually made of painted silk on a bamboo frame, with a silk string attached to it. Of all the art forms in the Chinese culture, kites are one of the well-known handicraft arts beaming with national characteristics, and the kite flying has become a favorite pastime among the people.

Kite flying is widespread in China especially in Beijing and Weifang which are both epicenters of kite manufacturing and flying. Kites are made in various styles by professional or amateur artists of different schools. Eulogized as China's kite capital the city of Weifang in the northern province of Shandong hosts an International Kite Fair and kite-flying tournament every spring just before the Qingming Festival. The event attracts numerous contestants from all over the world and a growing number of tourists from home and abroad.

The Categories and Making Craft of Chinese Kite

Generally, Chinese kites have two major categories: those with detachable wings and those with fixed wings. The former can be taken apart and packed in boxes. Easy to carry about, they make good presents. The second category refers to those with fixed, non-detachable frames; they fly better and higher, given a steady wind. Classified by designs and other specifications, there are no less than 300 varieties, including human figures, fish, insects, birds, and written characters. In size, they range from 304 metres to only 30 centimetres across.

As stated beforehand, the earliest Chinese kites were made of wood and called muyuan; they date as far back as the Warring States Period at least two millennia ago. After the invention of paper, kites began to be made of this new material called zhiyuan. During the Tang Dynasty, people began to fix on kites some bamboo strips which, when high in the air, would vibrate and ring in the breeze like a zheng (a stringed instrument). The kites made today in certain localities are fixed with silk strings or rubber bands to give out pleasant ringing in the wind.

It is not an easy job to make a kite that one can be proud of. For the frame, the right kind of bamboo must be selected. It should be thick and strong for a kite of large dimensions in order to stand the wind pressure. For miniature kites, on the other hand, thin bamboo strips are to be used. The second step in the making of a kite is the covering of the frame. This is normally done with paper, sometimes with silk. Silk kites are more durable and generally of higher artistic value. Painting of the kite (the third step) may be done in either of two ways. For mass-produced kites, pre-printed paper is used to cover the frames. Custom-made kites are painted manually after covering. Many of the designs bear messages of good luck; a pine tree and a crane, for example, mean longevity, bats and peaches wish you good fortune and a long life and so on.

The Social Function of the Kites

Be an important custom and good for health

Instead of being playthings, it was also believed that flying a kite and then letting it go meant apart from the pleasure in itself might send off one's bad luck and illness. This custom continues today. Every year before the Qingming festival Chinese would bring their families outside for a simple excursion. The important thing in the spring excursion may be flying kites. From the health point flying kites can treat cervical spondylosis and it can also alleviate social pressures from the mental aspect.

Drive the development of relative industry

In addition to individual significance, kite-flying is also a significant economic function. As we all known, kite is not only used to play but also decorate the house. According to this, the relative industry was appeared to meet the demand. It also pushes the economic and employed development.

Push the development of some cities

However, the influence of kites is not only on the income but also on the cultural and city development. The most outstanding example should be Weifang Kite Festival and kite in Weifang represents the development of Chinese kite culture. The well-known Weifang

Kite Festival has become an annual feature in the country. As the international festival, including political, economic, foreign affairs, cultural and sports activities, it has held 25 times. The Weifang International Kite Festival in 2005 had sold 12.5 million kites and brought 553 million yuan income. Small kite culture has pushed local economic development. The small city has established friendly and cooperative relations between economic and trade exchanges with 145 countries and regions. In 2006, the city has completed 115.6 billion yuan of gross domestic product. With the several years development, Weifang kites has become an important cultural industry from the individual amusement. Kite companies have reached than two or three hundred in the city and annual sales are more than 2 billion yuan.

Be an important bridge between China and the world

At present, the kite becomes the important bridge of economic and cultural communication between the China and world. It is believed that Chinese kites were introduced to N. Korea, Japan, Malaysia, Europe, America and some other countries. As early as two dozen years ago, a film entitled *The Kite* was jointly made by Chinese and French studios, which is a sing of Sino-French friendship through the "adventures" of a kite. Each year, Weifang International Kite Festival is held in April, and kite enthusiasts from all over the world take part and compete in the festival.

Words & Expressions

hub /hʌb/ *n.* （活动的）中心
flaunt /flɔ:nt/ *vt.* 炫耀，卖弄；无视，蔑视； *vi.* 炫耀；飘扬
harrier /ˈhæriə(r)/ *n.* 猎兔犬
hawk /hɔ:k/ *n.* 鹰，隼
epicenter /ˈepɪsentə(r)/ *n.* 中心
eulogize /ˈju:lədʒaɪz/ *vt.* 颂扬；称赞
tournament /ˈtʊənəmənt/ *n.* 锦标赛，联赛
contestant /kənˈtestənt/ *n.* 参赛者，竞争者；争辩者
detachable /dɪˈtætʃəbl/ *adj.* 可拆卸的，可分开的
millennia /mɪˈleniə/ *n.* 千年期；千周年纪念日（millennium 的复数）
vibrate /vaɪˈbreɪt/ *v.* （使）震动，（使）颤动
miniature /ˈmɪnətʃə(r)/ *adj.* 微型的，小型的
longevity /lɒnˈdʒevəti/ *n.* 寿命；长寿，持久
cervical /ˈsɜ:vɪk(ə)l/ *adj.* 颈的
spondylosis /ˌspɒndɪˈləʊsɪs/ *n.* 椎关节强硬

Notes

1. **Weifang International Kite Fair**: 潍坊风筝节于每年四月的第三个周六在潍坊举

行，有来自世界各地的 30 多个国家和地区参赛，是我国最早冠以"国际"并被国际社会承认的大型地方节会。从 1984 年，已成功举办过三十八届，其创立的"风筝牵线、文体搭台、经贸唱戏"的模式，被全国各地广为借鉴。

2. 在农村放风筝，一般都在田中进行。在种麦地区，麦子要过了清明才分蘖发棵，"清明到，麦秆叫"。据农业专家研究，分蘖前的麦子不怕踩，如踩的话，对发棵拔节有一定的促进作用。但分蘖后的麦子便不能再踩了，因为麦子在分蘖后，茎干均长成，如这时再到田中放风，会踏坏田禾，使麦子产量降低。而在产稻地区，清明是大忙时节了。所以，在广大农村中，放风筝的活动一般在清明前后即告尾声，最晚的也只到立夏为止。

3. 过去，我国各地在放风筝时还举行种种有趣的仪式。有的地方是在放飞前，拿着风筝在村中游行，并在村头摆上香案，由村中德高望重的老人带着村中男人举行祭祀仪式，以求风筝能够顺利上天，祈祝风调雨顺，五谷丰收，然后才能放飞风筝。有的在风筝上画上神像或贴上神马，选一吉日，由"童男子"放上天空，据说这样便可镇慑人间妖魔，以保一方太平。在有些地方，人们有灾或有疾病时便在风筝上写上自己的名字，待风筝放上天后剪断引线，让风筝随风飘去。

Reading Comprehension

Ⅰ. **Each piece of the following information is given in one of the paragraphs in the passage. Identify the paragraph from which the information is derived and put the corresponding number in the space provided.**

(   ) 1. As a folk art, the Chinese kite is usually made of painted silk on a bamboo frame, with a silk string attached to it.

(   ) 2. Classified by designs and other specifications, there are no less than 300 varieties, including human figures, fish, insects, birds, animals and written characters.

(   ) 3. The second step in the making of a kite is the covering of the frame.

(   ) 4. The well-known Weifang Kite Festival has become an annual feature in the country.

(   ) 5. At present, the kite becomes the important bridge of economic and cultural communication between the China and world.

Ⅱ. **Decide whether the statements are true (T) or false (F) according to the passage.**

(   ) 1. The earliest mention of a kite in ancient China dates back to the 6th century BC.

(   ) 2. Those with fixed wings can be taken apart and packed in boxes.

(   ) 3. After the invention of paper, kites began to be made of this new material called zhiyuan.

(   ) 4. During the Ming Dynasty, people began to fix on kites some bamboo strips which, when high in the air, would vibrate and ring in the breeze like a zheng (a stringed instrument).

(   ) 5. Each year, Weifang International Kite Festival is held in April, and kite enthusiasts from all over the world take part and compete in the festival.

III. Complete the sentences with the correct form of the words in the table.

eulogize	detach	miniature	longevity	alleviate
epicenter	entitle	handicraft	contestant	flaunt

1. With a history of dynasties and city-states, this cultural hub of Asian invention _____ a number of "firsts", including the invention of paper and kites.

2. Of all the art forms in the Chinese culture, kites are one of the well-known _____ arts beaming with national characteristics, and the kite flying has become a favorite pastime among the people.

3. Kite flying is widespread in China especially in Beijing and Weifang which are both _____ of kite manufacturing and flying.

4. _____ as China's kite capital the city of Weifang in the northern province of Shandong hosts an International Kite Fair and kite-flying tournament every spring just before Qingming.

5. The event attracts numerous _____ from all over the world and a growing number of tourists from home and abroad.

6. Generally, Chinese kites have two major categories: those with _____ wings and those with fixed wings.

7. For _____ kites, on the other hand, thin bamboo strips are to be used.

8. Many of the designs bear messages of good luck; a pine tree and a crane, for example, mean _____, bats and peaches wish you good fortune and a long life and so on.

9. From the health point flying kites can treat cervical spondylosis and it can also _____ social pressures from the mental aspect.

10. As early as two dozen years ago, a film _____ The Kite was jointly made by Chinese and French studios, which is a sing of Sino-French friendship through the "adventures" of a kite.

IV. Match the sentences in Section A with the English translation in Section B

Section A

1. 大约从唐代以后，中国风筝流传到朝鲜、日本、马来西亚等地，然后又流传到欧美等地区。

2. 根据设计和用途等分类，中国风筝有300多种，例如，人物、鱼、昆虫、鸟等。

3. 著名的"潍坊风筝节"已经成为中国每年一次的大型活动，每年四月吸引着国内外的大批风筝爱好者参加。

4. 中国最早的风筝木制而成，古称"木鸢"，至少可以追溯到2000多年前的战国时期。

5. 第二类风筝的飞翼是固定的，龙骨不能拆开，但是飞得更高、更好、更稳。

Section B

1. The earliest Chinese kites were made of wood and called muyuan (wooden kites); they date as far back as the Warring States Period at least two millennia ago.

2. The second category refers to those with fixed, non-detachable frames; they fly better and higher, given a steady wind.

3. Classified by designs and other specifications, there are no less than 300 varieties, including human figures, fish, insects, birds, and written characters.

4. In about Tang Dynasty, Chinese kites were introduced to N. Korea, Japan, Malaysia and then to Europe and America.

5. The well-known Weifang Kite Festival has become an annual feature in the country, drawing hundreds of participants each April from home and many foreign countries.

V. Translate the paragraph into Chinese.

Swallow-shaped kites are quite popular in Beijing. Craftsmen fashion them in many different ways. Some are strewed with peonies, bats and other auspicious poems to bring the owner good fortune. Kites made in Nantong are usually flown with whistles and rings. When they are flying in the sky, they vividly resemble a bevy of twittering birds, while the whistles and rings sound like guzheng (a plucked Chinese ancient 16~26 stinged zither). So the kite is named fengzheng in Chinese, literally meaning guzheng in the wind. Tianjin boasts the large variety of kites. With different unique and novel shapes, a larger kite can measure hundreds of meters while the smallest can be put in an envelope. Kites with soft wings in the shape of insects, goldfish, clouds and even a swallow linked with dozens of little swallows are all available, and each of these attractive kites reflects the consummate skill of the craftsman.

_____
_____
_____
_____

Development

VI. Discuss the following questions.

1. What is the process to make a kite?
2. What is the social function of the kites?

Text B 剪纸 Paper-cutting

One of China's most popular folk arts is paper-cutting. Archaeological finds trace the tradition back to the 6th century; it is supposed that the beginnings of paper cutting were even a few centuries earlier. Paper-cuttings are used for religious purposes, for decoration and as patterns. Today, paper-cuttings are chiefly used as decoration. They ornament walls, windows, doors, columns, mirrors, lamps and lanterns in homes and are also used for decoration on presents or are given as presents themselves. They have special significance at festivals. At the New Year's Festival, for example, entrances are decorated with paper-cutting which are supposed to bring good luck.

Of the folk art works, paper-cutting is the most participated. Often characterized by geographical regions, paper-cutting is rich with historical and cultural heritage. Even though it has only been two thousand years since the invention of paper, the cultural implication and art forms that paper-cutting represents goes back all the way to primitive society 6000~7000 years ago. The cultural value it carries far exceeds the value of art itself; it enriches the entire original Chinese art system, art formation and color structure, having deep impact on philosophy, aesthetics, history, ethnology, sociology and anthropology.

Today, great strides have been made in the art of paper-cutting in terms of the themes, patterns, cutting or engraving skills, mounting, and artisans or craftsmen, and many styles of paper-cutting have been developed with the passage of time. Everything can become the theme of paper-cutting, from people to the things that can be found in everyday life such as birds and flowers, animals and insects. In many parts of China, paper-cutting skill has become a must for women, old and young and the symbol of a clever mind and nimble fingers for Chinese ladies as a whole.

While paper-cutting remains popular in China today, especially during special events like weddings and Chinese New Year, paper-cutting art has developed into an entirely new art form independent of its paper-cutting roots. The attractiveness of paper-cutting art lies in the humble medium of paper, which is transformed into intricate, exotic and even three-dimensional designs due solely to the artist's skill and imagination.

In contemporary paper-cutting art, artists some times combine paper-cutting with other media and materials such as paint, installation and light boxes to create additional effects. But what remains at the core of the medium is the fashioning of elaborate patterns by the artist's bare hands, and the creative use of positive and negative space.

The Features of the Chinese Paper-cutting

With a vast territory and multi-ethnic population, Chinese folk paper-cutting bears distinct national and geographical features. In art style, northern China is more straightforward, unconstraint, and broad minded; while in the south, it's more exquisite and delicate, full of delight and witty. From the creators, the rural female folk artists use only a pair of scissors and paper to convey their conceptual figures and color effect which surpass time and space; while male-dominant career artists make paper carvings with superb delicacy and graciousness in a more realistic style and art language. From the functionality in social life, paper-cutting for embroidery patterns are given more emphasis on the outline for decorativeness; while cave window decoration gives more delicacy to the inner pattern to let in light. In general art style, each art work brings out a unique, personal touch of the author.

It is easy to learn about cutting a piece of paper but difficult to master it with perfection. One must grasp the knife in an upright fashion and press evenly on the paper with some strength. Flexibility is required but any hesitation or wiggling will lead to imprecision or damage the whole image. Engravers stress the cutting lines in several and there are four ideal but basic lines that they endeavor to master. They attempt to carve a circle like the moon, a straight line like a stem of wheat, a square like a brick, and jaggedly like the beard.

The Social Function of Paper-cutting

Express wishes

Paper-cutting is the Chinese traditional craft and can been seen everywhere now. People find hope and comfort in expressing wishes with paper cuttings. For example, for a wedding ceremony, red paper-cutting are a traditional and requires decoration on the tea set, the dressing table glass, and on other furniture. A big red paper character "Xi" (happiness) is a traditional must on the newlywed's door. Upon the birthday party of a senior, the character "Shou" represents longevity and will add delight to the whole celebration; while a pattern of plump children cuddling fish signifies that every year they will be abundant in wealth.

Promote the development of relative industry

Owing to the fact that the paper cutting has more application, relative cooperates had been set for several years. The paper-cutting industry includes material production, art design, product processing, paper-cutting exports. For example, the paper-cutting company in Wei county of Hebei province can product 300 000 sets of paper-cutting every year and sell half of the products to 40 countries and regions.

Enrich the people's life

Another important function of paper-cutting is that it has inherited Chinese culture. The paper-cutting art is liked by many people and they would like to learn and do paper-cutting works in their leisure time. In some provinces the cultural department has organize the paper-cutting corporation to enrich the residents' life and cultivate the awareness of traditional culture. For example, during the eighth Arts Festival of Wuhan in Hubei, the Chinese folk paper-cutting research had hold the exhibition which named "traditional culture come back" in 2007. This is the first time to list the paper-cutting in the Chinese arts festival. Paper-cutting is a worldwide cultural phenomenon. Chinese paper-cutting has a strong influence in Asia, like in Japan. The Tang Dynasty paper-cutting of relics still retained; in the southeast Asia which is the region of Buddhist culture, paper-cutting and paper carving of temple are both from China.

Words & Expressions

archaeological /ˌaːkiə'lɒdʒɪk(ə)l/ *adj.* 考古学的；考古学上的
ornament /'ɔːnəmənt/ *v.* 装饰，点缀
aesthetics /iːs'θetɪks; es'θetɪks/ *n.* 美学；美学理论；艺术美
ethnology /eθ'nɒlədʒi/ *n.* 人种学；人类文化学
anthropology /ˌænθrə'pɒlədʒi/ *n.* 人类学
engrave /ɪn'ɡreɪv/ *v.* 雕刻（文字，图案）
mount /maʊnt/ *v.* 镶嵌，裱贴，安置
nimble /'nɪmbl/ *adj.* （行动）灵活的；（头脑）聪敏的
intricate /'ɪntrɪkət; 'ɪntrɪkɪt/ *adj.* 错综复杂的；难理解的，难学会的
unconstraint /ˌʌnkən'streɪnt/ *n.* 无拘无束，自由自在
exquisite /ɪk'skwɪzɪt; 'ekskwɪzɪt/ *adj.* 精致的，精美的；剧烈的；细致的，有鉴赏力的
graciousness /'ɡreɪʃəsnəs/ *n.* 亲切，和蔼；好心
embroidery /ɪm'brɔɪdəri/ *n.* 刺绣技法，刺绣活儿；绣花，刺绣品
wiggle /'wɪɡ(ə)l/ *v.* （使）扭动，摆动
cuddle /'kʌd(ə)l/ *v.* 搂抱，拥抱；紧靠…而坐(或躺)，依偎
relics /'relɪks/ *n.* 遗迹；遗骸；纪念物（relic 的复数）

Notes

剪纸艺术流传面之广、数量之大、样式之多、基础之深比任何一种艺术都更加突出。在各种民俗活动中，它无时不在、无处不有，附丽于生活，充实了生活，以它特

有的方式默默地唤起人们对生命的追求，对生活的信念，对国富民康的企盼；它将人们平凡的生活点缀得如此瑰丽多姿，充分寄托和体现了中华民族对真善美的追求和向往。如今，剪纸的天地更为广阔了，它早已走出了庄户人家的小院，走入现代设计的广阔天地，在产品包装设计、商标广告、室内装饰、服装设计、书装、邮票设计、报刊题花、连环画、舞台美术、动画、影视等各个方面都有它的倩影；它也走向世界，名扬四海，成为全人类的文化财富与艺术瑰宝。随着历史的进程许多民族的、传统的东西被渐渐淡化。然而，真正文明的标志应是传统文化和现代文化并存，共同发展。愿这棵古老的艺术之树常绿常新。

Reading Comprehension

Ⅰ. Each piece of the following information is given in one of the paragraphs in the passage. Identify the paragraph from which the information is derived and put the corresponding number in the space provided.

(　　) 1. Paper-cuttings are used for religious purposes, for decoration and as patterns.

(　　) 2. Today, great strides have been made in the art of paper-cutting in terms of the themes, patterns, cutting or engraving skills, mounting, and artisans or craftsmen.

(　　) 3. In contemporary paper-cutting art, artists sometimes combine paper-cutting with other media and materials such as paint, installation and light boxes to create additional effects.

(　　) 4. With a vast territory and multi-ethnic population, Chinese folk paper-cutting bears distinct national and geographical features.

(　　) 5. A pattern of plump children cuddling fish signifies that every year they will be abundant in wealth.

Ⅱ. Decide whether the statements are true (T) or false (F) according to the passage.

(　　) 1. They ornament walls, windows, doors, columns, mirrors, lamps and lanterns in homes and are also used for decoration on presents or are given as presents themselves.

(　　) 2. Even though it has only been two thousand years since the invention of paper, the cultural implication and art forms that paper-cutting represents goes back all the way to primitive society 3000~5000 years ago.

(　　) 3. In art style, southern China is more straightforward, unconstraint, and broad minded; while in the north, it's more exquisite and delicate, full of delight and witty.

(　　) 4. Flexibility is required but any hesitation or wiggling will lead to imprecision or damage the whole image.

(　　) 5. The paper-cutting industry includes material production, art design, product processing, paper-cutting exports.

Development

III. Discuss the following questions.

1. What are the features of the Chinese paper-cutting?
2. What is the social function of paper-cutting?

Text C 皮影戏 Shadow Puppetry

Shadow Puppetry, or Shadow Play, was very popular during the Tang and Song Dynasties in many parts of China. Shadow Puppets were first made of paper sculpture, later from the leather of donkeys or oxen. That's why their Chinese name is piying, which means shadows of leather.

Shadow generally includes shadow props and leather-silhouette shows. The former belongs to the category of arts and crafts and the latter belongs to the category of drama.

It has the characters of both graphic art and theatrical performance, with the extension to literature and the dependence on music; it becomes a comprehensive form of folk art which integrates painting, sculpture, literature, music, dance and performance.

The shadow mainly absorbs the methods from paper-cutting modeling, meanwhile borrowing the hollow-out transparent effects from paper-cutting for window decoration, and integrating the morphological characteristics from drama facial make-up, the murals, the sculpture, the stone relief, with unity of form and spirit lively portrayed as roles of sheng (young male role), dan (young female role), jing (painted face), chou (comedian) in the plays. Shadow puppets are more developed on the side face, 50% faces developed for the faithful, 70% faces developed for the traitor, and a few special faces developed on the front. Sculptors grasp the most important features of the characters for appropriate exaggeration by fully using the means of positive carving and intaglio, with positive carving to express the pure features of decent images, and intaglio to express the ugliness or ferocity of Jing (painted face) and chou (comedian). In the Song Dynasty, Nai Deweng's *Ducheng Jisheng (The Best of the Capital City)* mentioned that "Those who are loyal are carved with good looks, and those who are evil the ugly appearances, implying praise and derogation in it".

Shadow is a two-dimensional art, and it is performed through light and shadow. Unlike a movie, which can be shown by montage, freeze-frame, camera propulsion, close-up, etc. to reveal the inner thoughts of the characters, nor is it like a traditional Chinese opera, which can be expressed through the gestures and facial expressions of the actors, it can only be expressed by the actions of the shadow puppets and the singing of the background. Therefore, it is a special kind of screen art.

The shadow plays with "the development with the shadow" and "the development with the light". The shadow is to make full use of the principle of photo lithography to make the artistic images vivid, so the distance between the images and the screen is properly controlled, creating the effect of virtual reality. In order to create a more pleasing aesthetic effect for the script, the shadow performers have also created a number of methods to create unique stunt effects, showing such scenes as flying into the sky and drilling into the earth, stealthy deformation, smoking and firing, mounting the clouds and riding the mist, changes of gods and ghosts, splitting mountains or deforming the sea, coupled with a variety of acousto-optic effects, enough to make modern people feel refreshed.

Before the opera, there was a puppet play. Shadow is a puppet play with the functions to eliminate the evil spirits, reward the gods and send gods off. It was said that what the alchemist Shaoweng played for Emperor Wudi of the Han Dynasty was witchcraft. It was also believed that the description of Emperor Tang Mingwang's meeting with Yang Guifei after death in Bai Juyi's *The Song of Everlasting Sorrow* was the basis for the appearance of shadow plays at that time. Wang Hao's description in *Lin Tian Xu Lu (Records of the Forests and Farmlands)* in Yuan Dynasty meant the same, "to perform with puppets and wood in the plays while decorated with colorful fancy paper, to tell the stories, to pray for good luck and to drive away the evil spirits." This function still existed till Ming and Qing Dynasties.

In the Qing Dynasty, the shadow also experienced several ups and downs because of the nature of the puppet play. First, during the time of Jiaqing under the reign of Renzong, as a result of a civil riot, it was said that the shadow artists could be turned into "heavenly

generals & soldiers" to help the people, so that the government authorities raided the city's shadow troupes and captured artists, making the shadow arts almost perish. At the end of the Qing Dynasty, people's livelihood was low, riots sprung up frequently, and there was a rise of White Lotus Society. The Qing government arrested the shadow entertainers on the charge of "abstruse lamp bandits" by saying that they would use paper to entertain evil spirits and revolt. Even at the time of Emperor Guang Xu's death, he issued a notice banning the performance of shadow plays, saying that "the state is in great trouble and the people have no good nature. If they sing and perform again, they will arouse greater riots."

The education functions are as follows: firstly, shadow serves for religious spread; the other is the social responsibility to illuminate and strengthen social ethics and justice. Shadow puppets serve to preach dogma. The first is to spread the thoughts of Buddhism. "Lantern Folk Talk" and "Hanging Lantern, Preaching" in the Song Dynasty are all to let the general public bathe in the well-being of the Buddha. Later, shadow play was called "Taoist shadow" in some places. Taoist roamed the world and preached all over the country when singing in the form of shadow, followed by patterns and plots. The shadow play also regards the purification of social atmosphere as its own responsibility: to talk about the Romance of History and to distinguish loyalty from traitors, to combine praise and demoralization, to spread Confucian loyalty, filial piety, to illuminate ethics. And it tells folk legends and stories, elaborates joys and sorrows, and exhorts good deeds, which is full of civilized social functions. Even in the countryside where culture is inaccessible, ordinary people are able to get orthodox education after watching the shadow.

Shadow play has deep root in the folk. It makes a serious theme more common and a major theme understandable. According to *Notes on Yenching's Age*, the performance of the shadow is very vivid with the intricate and moving plots. On hearing the sad songs, some old women often can not help but shed tears. This shows that the appeal of shadow play is very strong. Shadow plays are always closely linked to rural production and life. Puppets for the day and shadow singing for the night not only bring people lively and active folk life, enrich people's interest in life, but also become the media for people to communicate with.

Shadow is a comprehensive art. It consists of the qualities of graphic plastic art, performance accompaniment and script, and the qualities of opera music, so it reflects the historical development process of folk art. Shadow is a transparent graphic art. The characters are characterized by both shapes and spirits. There are also recognizable symbols on the costumes of the characters. The age of the character and the needs of the plot must be combined and coordinated with different stubble and bodies. The shadow makes full use of the principle of light and shadow, the white screen and carving special images to break through the limits of time and space, cross the sea and drill into the earth.

Words & Expressions

silhouette /ˌsɪluˈet/ n. 轮廓，剪影
morphological /ˌmɔːfəˈlɒdʒɪkl/ adj. 形态学的
mural /ˈmjʊərəl/ n. 壁画
intaglio /ɪnˈtɑːliəʊ/ n. 凹雕；凹雕玉石；凹雕术
ferocity /fəˈrɒsəti/ n. 凶猛；残忍；暴行
derogation /ˌderəˈɡeɪʃn/ n. 毁损，减损；堕落
montage /ˌmɒnˈtɑːʒ; ˈmɒntɑːʒ/ n. 蒙太奇（电影的基本结构手段和叙事方式）
propulsion /prəˈpʌlʃn/ n. 推进；推进力
photolithography /ˌfəʊtəlɪˈθɒɡrəfi/ n. 影印石版术；照相平印术
stealthy /ˈstelθi/ adj. 鬼鬼祟祟的；秘密的
deformation /ˌdiːfɔːˈmeɪʃn/ n. 变形
acousto-optic /əˌkuːstəʊˈɒptɪk(əl)/ adj. 声光的
alchemist /ˈælkəmɪst/ n. 炼金术士
troupe /truːp/ n. 巡回演出团
perish /ˈperɪʃ/ v. 湮灭，毁灭
abstruse /əbˈstruːs/ adj. 深奥的；难懂的
bandit /ˈbændɪt/ n. 强盗，土匪；恶棍
revolt /rɪˈvəʊlt/ n. 叛乱，造反
illuminate /ɪˈluːmɪneɪt/ v. 阐明，解释
dogma /ˈdɒɡmə/ n. 教条，信条，教义
roam /rəʊm/ vi. 漫游，漫步；流浪；vt. 在…漫步，漫游；在…流浪
demoralization /dɪˌmɒrəlaɪˈzeɪʃn/ n. 堕落；道德败坏；士气低落
filial /ˈfɪliəl/ adj. 孝顺的
piety /ˈpaɪəti/ n. 虔诚，虔敬
exhort /ɪɡˈzɔːt/ vt. 忠告；劝诫；vi. 劝告

orthodox /'ɔːθədɒks/ adj.（观念、方法或行为）传统的，正统的
stubble/'stʌbl/ n. 胡子茬，发茬，须茬

Notes

1. Shadow generally includes shadow props and leather-silhouette shows. The former belongs to the category of arts and crafts and the latter belongs to the category of drama.
一般所说的皮影，包括皮影道具和皮影戏。前者属于工艺美术的范畴，后者属于戏剧的范畴。

2. In the Song Dynasty, Nai Deweng's *Ducheng Jisheng (The Best of the Capital City)* mentioned that "Those who are loyal are carved with good looks, and those who are evil the ugly appearances, implying praise and derogation in it."
宋代耐得翁在《都城纪胜》提到："公忠者雕以正貌，奸邪者予以丑貌，盖亦寓褒贬于其间耳。"

3. *The Song of Everlasting Sorrow* was the basis for the appearance of shadow plays at that time.
白居易之《长恨歌》中出现的唐明皇与杨贵妃死后相聚的描述就是当时皮影戏出现的依据。

4. Wang Hao's description in *Lin Tian Xu Lu (Records of the Forests and Farmlands)* in Yuan Dynasty meant the same, "to perform with puppets and wood in the plays while decorated with colorful fancy paper, to tell the stories, to pray for good luck and to drive away the evil spirits." This function still existed till Ming and Qing Dynasties.
元代的汪颢《林田叙录》云："傀儡牵木作戏，影戏彩纸斑斓，敷陈故事祈福辟禳。"

Reading Comprehension

I. Each piece of the following information is given in one of the paragraphs in the passage. Identify the paragraph from which the information is derived and put the corresponding number in the space provided.

(　　) 1. It becomes a comprehensive form of folk art which integrates painting, sculpture, literature, music, dance and performance.

(　　) 2. Shadow is a two-dimensional art, and it is performed through light and shadow.

(　　) 3. In the Qing Dynasty, the shadow also experienced several ups and downs because of the nature of the puppet play.

(　　) 4. The shadow play also regards the purification of social atmosphere as its own responsibility.

(　　) 5. It consists of the qualities of graphic plastic art, performance accompaniment and script, and the qualities of opera music.

II. **Decide whether the statements are true (T) or false (F) according to the passage.**

(   ) 1. Shadow generally includes leather-silhouette shows and shadow props. The former belongs to the category of arts and crafts and the latter belongs to the category of drama.

(   ) 2. Shadow puppets are more developed on the side face, 70% faces developed for the faithful, 50% faces developed for the traitor.

(   ) 3. It was said that what the alchemist Shaoweng played for Emperor Wudi of the Han Dynasty was witchcraft.

(   ) 4. The education functions are as follows: firstly, shadow serves for religious propaganda; the other is the social responsibility to illuminate and strengthen social ethics and justice.

(   ) 5. Shadow plays are always closely linked to rural production and life.

Development

III. **Discuss the following questions.**

1. What are the artistic features of the shadow puppets?
2. What are the functions of the shadow puppets?

第六章 茶

Chapter 6　Tea

Text A　茶之识　About Tea

Tea is a widely cultivated shrub having glossy green leaves and fragrant white flowers. Tea, beverage produced by steeping in freshly boiled water the young leaves and leaf buds of the tea plant, Camellia sinensis, a member of the family Theaceae, which contains about 40 genera of trees and shrubs.

Did tea plant originate from China or India? There has been a long argument about this question as wild tea plants have been both found in China and in India. But now it seems that China is more possible to be its country of origin. The reason is that tea plant, according to the modern botanical theory, has a history of at least 60 million years, much long before the combination of the Indian Plate into the Eurasian, which happened about 40 million years ago. If there is possibility that tea plant first grew in Indian Subcontinent there must be a fact that before it joined the Eurasian Plate it had carried tea plants on the way from Africa to Asia. And to prove this there is only one way: to find wild tea plant in Madagascar Island or Eastern Africa where the Indian Plate was from. But up to now there has been no wild tea plant to be found in the two regions except the transplanted ones. This suggests that the wild tea plants found in India must be spread there from southwestern China. Since there have been more and more large old wild tea trees to be found in southwestern China, it is more reasonable that China is the hometown of tea.

As far as the genesis of tea culture is concerned, it refers to when, where and by whom it was first drunk or eaten. Now that there are only two countries in the world where wild tea trees have been found, the genesis of tea culture must emerge in one of them. Considering that it was only in 1824 that wild tea plant was first found in India whereas as early as the eighth century a treatise on tea had been produced in China. It goes without saying that China is, apart from the birthplace of tea tree, the cradle of tea culture.

About the genesis of tea culture, it is said in *Cha Jing* (*The Classic of Tea*) by Lu Yu that tea drink originated from Divine Husbandman. And other legends describe the story as: one day Divine Husbandman, who was believed to taste kinds of herbs and thereby became the ancestor of Chinese medicine, ate by mistake a very poisonous herb and became serious ill. When he laid dying under an unknown tree some leaves fell into his mouth and he chewed and swallowed them. Then a miracle happened and he got better and better and at last survived the misfortune. Thereafter, he used that kind of leave to cure deceases of people. This magical tree was later called "tea".

If the story is true, it means that tea culture in China has a history of about 5000 years. However, so far except the legend itself there has been no evidence to prove such a history in China but what we are sure is that Chinese people began to make use of tea at least before the Qin Dynasty, because in a classical document called Er Ya which was compiled at the end of the Warring States Period or the beginning of the Han Dynasty, tea, though it was called jia at that time, is mentioned. Both the legend and some documents indicate that tea was first used as medicine. For example, in Shennong's Classic of Materia Medica, the oldest medical classic in Chin which was believed to came into being in the late Pre-Qin Period or the early Han Dynasty, tea's medical properties and functions were introduced. Apart from being used as medicine, tea was also used as food in the early times. Ancient literature shows that people in southern China have widely mixed tea with kinds of grains or vegetables to make "tea porridge" or "tea cake".

The first clear record of tea used as a drink is a poem from the Western Jin Dynasty, On a Tower in Chengdu by Zhang Zai, in which we read, "supreme is tea among the six fragrances, in the nine continents of China its smell diffuses". This indicates that in the Western Jin Dynasty tea had become a popular drink. However unearthed relics show that tea drink came into being might much earlier than this time. In documents from the Tomb of Xin Zhui of the Western Han Dynasty the word "tea" appear four times and a painting from the same tomb is identified as *Portrait of a Lady Sewing Tea*. What's more, in a literary work titled *A Bond of Enslavement* by Wang Bao in the Western Han Dynasty the duties of the servant include buying tea-leaves and boiling tea water. This shows that tea drinking had already prevailed at the beginning of the Han Dynasty, at least among the upper classes.

Archaeological discoveries proved that tea came from southwestern China, in provinces like Yunnan, Guizhou and Sichuan, as the core area of cultivation. As time went by, tea cultivation became popular across the world, spreading to every corner of the globe.

According to *The classic of Tea*, the first monograph that comprehensively introduces tea written by Lu Yu, tea, as a drink, originated with Shennong and was popularized by Ji Dan (one of the founding figures of the Zhou Dynasty). Before and during the Han Dynasty, what is now Sichuan Province is already a center of tea business. Some places were named after tea, and tea markets developed in different regions. However, at that time, tea was made of wild leaves; the tea tree planting was not popularized until the Tang Dynasty. It was after *Cha Jing*'s publication that the Tang Dynasty saw rapid development of tea cultivation.

The cultivation gradually spread from its original regions in south China to over so Miles and prefectures, including areas in provinces of Henan, Shaanxi and Gansu in northern and northwestern China. This rapid development called for the introduction of more technology in tea cultivation. Therefore, it gave rise to *Sishi Zuanyao* (*Cultivation in Four Seasons*), a book publicized between the late Tang Dynasty and the period of the Five Dynasties, which offered a detailed introduction to selection of site, management of tea gardens, cultivation of tea trees and storage of tea seeds, etc..

A step-by-step method of tea cultivation is illustrated in *Sishi Zuanyao*, prior to any other book in detailed introduction of tea cultivation and tea seeds storage in Chinese history. The book mentioned that *Cha Jing* is another classic work written on tea. According to Lu Yu, if tea leaves were collected at the wrong time, processed in a wrong way or mixed with other stuff, they would do harm to people's health. It was in sunny days during lunar February, March and April, with dew in tea leaves, that were the best timing to pick them along the Yangtze River Valley. Additionally, soil conditions might dominate when and how to pick tea leaves. For those growing on barren and weedy ground, leaves should be picked from three to five trees. Another be picked from the best one out of every influential factor is the weather—tea leaves couldn't be collected on rainy and cloudy days. Cha Jing also introduced new ways to process tea leaves Before the book, tea was made the same way as that of vegetables, and people drank tea with leaves.

Chinese people are the first in the world to drink tea, and, with countless efforts, different kinds of tea have been cultivated, thus forming the unique tea culture. This is not only a valuable experience for the Chinese people but also a great treasure for the world.

The Chinese famous tea or The Ten Great Chinese Teas are the ten most notable Chinese teas. Below is a list of ten popular teas of China (Table 6.1).

Table 6.1 Varieties of Tea

Chinese	English	Region	Type
西湖龙井	Longjing tea (also spelled Lungching; Dragonwell)	Hangzhou, Zhejiang	Green tea
洞庭碧螺春	Biluochun tea (also spelled Pi Lou Chun) or Dongding Green Spiral	Suzhou, Jiangsu	Green tea
安溪铁观音	Anxi Tieguanyin tea	Anxi, Fujian	Oolong tea
黄山毛峰	Huangshan Maofeng tea	Huangshan, Anhui	Green tea
武夷岩茶/大红袍	Wuyi Mountain Rock or Da Hong Pao (Big Red Robe) tea	Wuyi, Fujian	Oolong tea
君山银针	Junshan Yinzhen (Jun Mountain Silver Needle)	Yueyang, Hunan	Yellow tea
祁门红茶	Keemun Black tea	Qimen, Anhui	Black tea

(续)

Chinese	English	Region	Type
六安瓜片	Lu'an Melon Seed tea	Jinzhai, Anhui	Green tea
云南普洱	Yunnan Puer	Puer (Simao), Yunnan	Post-fermented teaPuer
白毫银针	Baihao Yinzhen (White Tip Silver Needle)	Fuding, Fujian	White tea

Longjing Tea

Longjing tea sometimes called by its literal translated name Dragon Well tea, is a variety of pan-roasted greentea from the area of Longjing Village near Hangzhou in Zhejiang Province, China. It is produced mostly by hand and renowned for its high quality, earning it the China Famous Tea title.

Like most other Chinese green tea, Longjing tea leaves are roasted early in processing (after picking) to stop the natural oxidation process, which is a part of creating black and oolong teas. The actions of these enzymes are stopped by "firing" (heating in pans) or by steaming the leaves before they completely dry out. As is the case with other green teas (and white teas), Longjing tea leaves experience minimal oxidation. When steeped, the tea produces a yellow-green color. The tea contains vitamin C, amino acids and like most finer Chinese green teas, has one of the highest concentrations of catechins among teas.

For best infusion results, water at around 75~80 ℃ or 167~176 °F should be used to brew the tea leaves. Although it is common practice nowadays to steep Longjing tea in porcelain or glassware, the real taste profile of a finer Longjing is achieved only by using a genuine, slightly porous, Yixing clay teapot, which since the beginning, was popular exactly for preparing green tea well.

The tea can be very expensive, and the prices depend on the varieties, of which there are many. Longjing is divided into 6 grades: superior and then 1 down to 5. Infused leaves are a good indicator of quality, which is characterized by maturity and uniformity of the shoots harvested for processing. High quality Longjing teas produce tender, whole leaves that are uniform in appearance. Lower quality varieties may vary in color from bluish to deep green after steeping. Before infusion, higher quality Longjing teas have a very tight, flat shape and light green color. A study by Wang and Ruan found that one aspect of the perceived low quality of Longjing teas was a higher concentration of chlorophyll, producing a darker green color. The study revealed that free amino acids and the amine concentration contribute positively to what is perceived as a good taste.

There are various definitions of Longjing, however a common definition is that authentic Longjing at least has to come from Zhejiang province in China, with the most conservative definition restrict the type to the various villages and plantations in the West Lake area in Hangzhou. It can also be defined as any tea grown within the Xihu District. A large majority of Longjing tea on the market however is actually not from Hangzhou. Many of these inauthentic Longjing teas are produced in provinces such as Yunnan,

Guizhou, Sichuan, and Guangdong. However credible sellers may sometimes provide anti-fake labels or openly state that the tea is not from Zhejiang.

Experienced drinkers may be able to tell if Longjing is authentic by taste and smell. The aroma and flavors of the in authentic Longjing teas are not as complex, or long-lasting as the authentic tea. These teas, although similar in appearance, are mild in flavor and aroma and do not have the long-lasting aftertaste of the original.

Some tea makers take fresh tea leaves produced in Yunnan, Guizhou and Sichuan provinces and process them using Longjing tea techniques; and some merchants mix a small amount of high-grade with low-grade tea, and sell it as expensive high-grade.

Pu-erh Tea

Pu-erh or Pu'er is a variety of fermented tea produced in the Yunnan province, China, and named after Pu'er City. Fermentation in the context of tea production involves microbial fermentation and oxidation of the tea leaves, after they have been dried and rolled. This process is a Chinese specialty and produces tea known as heicha (黑茶), commonly translated as dark, or black tea. This type of tea is different from what in the West is known as "black tea", which in China is called "hongcha" (红茶) i.e. "red tea". The best known variety of this category of tea is pu'er from Yunnan Province, named after the trading post for dark tea during imperial China.

Pu'er traditionally begins as a raw product known as "rough" maocha (毛茶) and can be sold in this form or pressed into a number of shapes and sold as "raw" shengcha (生茶). Both of these forms then undergo the complex process of gradual fermentation and maturation with time. The wodui (渥堆) fermentation process developed in 1973 by the Kunming Tea Factory created a new type of pu'er tea. This process involves an accelerated fermentation into "ripe" shucha (熟茶) which is then stored loose or pressed into various shapes. The fermentation process was adopted at the Menghai Tea Factory shortly after and technically developed there. The legitimacy of shucha is disputed by some traditionalists in contrast to aged teas. All types of pu'er can be stored to mature before consumption, which is why it is commonly labelled with the year and region of production.

Darkening tea leaves to trade with ethnic groups at the borders has a long history in China. These crude teas were of various origins and were meant to below cost. Darkened tea, or heicha, is still the major beverage for the ethnic groups in the southwestern borders and, until the early 1990s, was the third major tea category produced by China mainly for this market segment.

Black Tea

Popular varieties of black tea include Assam, Nepal, Darjeeling, Nilgiri, Keemun and Ceylon teas. Many of the active substances in black tea do not develop at temperatures lower than 90℃. As a result, black tea in the West is usually steeped in water near its boiling point, at around 99℃. The most common fault when making black tea is to use water at too low temperature. Since boiling point drops with increasing altitude, it is difficult to brew black tea properly in mountainous areas. Warming the tea pot before steeping is critical at any elevation.

Western black teas are usually brewed for about four minutes and are usually not allowed to steep for less than 30 seconds or more than about five minutes (a process known as brewing or mashing in Britain). In many regions of the world, however, actively boiling water is used and the tea is often stewed. In India, black tea is often boiled for fifteen minutes or longer to make Masala chai, as a strong brew is preferred. Tea should be strained while serving.

A food safety management group of the International Organization for Standardization (ISO) has published a standard for preparing a cup of tea (ISO 3103: Tea—Preparation of liquor for use in sensory tests), primarily intended for standardizing preparation for comparison and rating purposes.

Green Tea

In regions of the world that prefer mild beverages, such as the West and Far East, green tea should be steeped in water around 80 to 85℃ (176 to 185°F), the higher the quality of the leaves the lower the temperature. Regions such as North Africa or Central Asia prefer a bitter tea, and hotter water is used. In Morocco, green tea is steeped in boiling water for 15 minutes.

The container in which green tea is steeped is often warmed beforehand to prevent premature cooling. High-quality green and white teas can have new water added as many as five or more times, depending on variety, at increasingly higher temperatures.

Oolong Tea

Oolong tea should be brewed around 82℃ to 96℃, with the brewing vessel warmed before pouring the water. Yixing purple clay teapots are the traditional brewing-vessel for oolong tea which can be brewed multiple times from the same leaves, unlike green tea, seeming to improve with reuse. In the Chinese Gongfu tea ceremony, the first brew is discarded, as it is considered a rinse of leaves rather than a proper brew.

Some teas, especially green teas and delicate oolong teas, are steeped for shorter periods, sometimes less than 30 seconds. Using a tea strainer separates the leaves from the water at the end of the brewing time if a tea bag is not being used. However, the black Darjeeling tea, a premium Indian tea, needs a longer than average steeping time. Elevation and time of harvest offer varying taste profiles, proper storage and water quality also have a large impact on taste.

shrub /ʃrʌb/ *n*. 灌木，灌木丛

camellia /kə'miːlɪə/ *n.* 山茶，山茶花，山茶属
theaceae /'θiːəsiˌiː/ *n.* 茶科，［植］山茶科
sinensis /si'nen.sis/ *n.* 虫草菌丝
diffuse /dɪ'fjuːz/ *v.* 扩散，弥漫，减弱，平息（不良情绪或局面），传播，散布；*adj.* 扩散的，弥漫的，难解的，冗长的
infuse /ɪn'fjuːz/ *v.* 冲泡（茶、药草等），浸渍，输注（药物等）
originate from 发源于

Tea is a widely cultivated shrub (Camellia sinensis of the family Theaceae, the tea family) native to China, northern India, and southeastern Asia and having glossy green leaves and fragrant white flowers.

茶是一种广泛种植的灌木（茶科山茶花，茶科），原产于中国、印度北部和东南亚，有光泽的绿叶和芳香的白花。

Reading Comprehension

I. Each piece of the following information is given in one of the paragraphs in the passage. Identify the paragraph from which the information is derived and put the corresponding number in the space provided.

(　　) 1. The production of oolong tea for export may begin from Fujian.

(　　) 2. By the end of the 14th century, the more naturalistic "loose leaf" form had become a popular household product.

(　　) 3. Gongfu tea ceremony literally means "making tea with skill".

(　　) 4. Distilled or extremely soft water should never be used for making tea as this form of water lacks minerals.

(　　) 5. Tea masters in China and other Asian tea cultures study for years to perfect this method.

II. Decide whether the statements are true (T) or false (F) according to the passage.

(　　) 1. Extremely soft water will negatively affect the flavor of the tea, thus it should never be used for making tea.

(　　) 2. All teas, loose tea, coarse tea, and powdered tea have coexisted for short periods with the "imperially appointed compressed form".

(　　) 3. In Gongfu tea ceremony, tea brewing tray is one of the main items.

(　　) 4. A tea pet is usually made of the different clay from tea pot.

(　　) 5. Gongfu tea ceremony is applied popularly by some teashops with tea of Chinese origins.

Language Focus

III. Complete the sentences with the correct form of the words in the table.

maximize	imperially	compressed	export	scholar
scent	ceremony	distilled	sizzling	brew

1. Each member of OPEC would seek to _____ its own production.
2. He _____ a pot of coffee.
3. The three original books have been _____ into one book.
4. A police dog picked up the murderer's _____.
5. The whisky had been _____ in 1926 and sat quietly maturing until 1987.
6. There is a _____ of prayer and flagellation before the dancing begins.
7. Kingdon's broad experience, as writer and _____, suffuses this important book.
8. As the domestic market becomes saturated, firms begin to _____ the product.
9. The smell of _____ steak makes my mouth water.
10. The _____ gallon was standardized legally throughout the British Empire.

IV. Match the sentences in Section A with the English translation in Section B.

Section A

1. 日本的茶叶生产仿效中国模式，开始于 12 世纪最终演变成为日本特有的茶艺，但仅限于日本的政治和军事精英阶级。
2. 本质上讲，"功夫茶"能带给人清香醇美、心旷神怡。
3. 煮制功夫茶时需注意用水。
4. 在煮制功夫茶时，必须保证茶达到并维持最佳温度。
5. 中国传统上一直重视茶叶的品质。

Section B

1. Attention to tea making quality has been a classic Chinese tradition.
2. In Japan, tea production began in the 12th century following Chinese models, and eventually evolved into the Japanese tea ceremony, meant to be exclusive to political and military elites.
3. In essence, what is desired in Gongfu tea is a brew that tastes good and is satisfying to the soul.
4. Water should be given careful consideration when conducting Gongfu tea.
5. During the process of Gongfu tea, an optimal temperature of tea must be reached and maintained.

V. Translate the paragraph into Chinese.

The Gongfu tea ceremony is a kind of Chinese tea ceremony, involving the ritual preparation and presentation of tea. It is probably based on the tea preparation approaches originated in Fujian and the Chaoshan area of eastern Guangdong. The term literally means "making tea with skill". Today, the approach is used popularly by teashops carrying tea of Chinese origins, and by tea connoisseurs as a way to maximize the taste of a tea selection, especially a finer one.

___

Development

VI. Discuss the following questions.

1. What are the characteristics of Gongfu tea ceremony?
2. Do you have more insights into the influence of Chinese tea ceremony?

Text B 茶之史 History of Tea

Chinese tea culture refers to how tea is prepared as well as the occasions when people consume tea in China. Tea culture in China differs from that in European countries like Britain and other Asian countries like Japan, Korea, Vietnam in preparation, taste, and occasion when it is consumed. Tea is still consumed regularly, both on casual and formal occasions. In addition to being a popular beverage, it is used in traditional Chinese medicine as well as in Chinese cuisine.

The concept of tea culture is referred to in Chinese as chayi (the art of drinking tea), or cha wenhua (tea culture). The word cha (茶) denotes the beverage that is derived from Camellia sinensis, the tea plant. Prior to the 8th century BC, tea was known collectively under the term "荼" (tu) along with a great number of other bitter plants. These two Chinese characters are identical, with the exception of an additional horizontal stroke in the Chinese lettering 茶, which translates to tea. The older character is made up of the radical 艸 (cao) in its reduced form of 艹 and the character 余 (yu), which gives the phonetic cue.

Tea culture in the Tang, Song, Ming and Qing Dynasties

As tea plants grew first in southern China, needless to say, tea culture was generated and became popular first in the south. But when the Beijing-Hangzhou Great Canal was constructed in the Sui Dynasty the situation was changed. The canal connected the south and the north through which products of the south, including tea-leaves, were continuously transported to the north, and the tea culture correspondingly spread from southern China to northern China. Because of this, tea culture, together with other cultures, became prosperous in the Tang Dynasty.

The area of tea plantation and thereby the tea production were greatly increased. According to modern study about tea culture in China. The tea plantation in the Tang Dynasty had spread to seventy six cantons including now Sichuan, Chongqing, Shaanxi, Hunan, Hubei, Guangdong, Fujian, Yunnan, Guizhou, Zhejiang, Jiangsu, Jiangxi, Anhui and Henan, etc..

Different tea cultures had evolved in different social strata or social groups. Alcoholic drinking was prohibited in Buddhist temple, and this made tea drinking particularly popular among monks, as it had no degenerating effect and was regarded promoting Buddhist spirit. So monastic tea culture developed fast in the Tang Dynasty. Meanwhile, high quality of tea-leaves, luxury of tea sets, fastidiousness and rituality of tea drinking characterized the aulic tea culture. Among literati tea was personified with kinds of virtues and so more than three hundred poems had been written by over one hundred poets to praise tea during the Tang Dynasty. And among populace tea drink was widely used to entertain visitors or used as sacrifice to gods or ancestral spirits.

A monograph on tea had been written, which is the famous *The Classic of Tea*. In this book the author, Lu Yu, introduced tea about its origination, its picking utensils and methods, its making process and skills, its boiling, storing and drinking wares, its boiling and drinking process, its stories and anecdotes, its producing places, etc. We can say it is an all-round summary of the tea culture of that time. Tea plants, tea products and tea culture began to spread to other countries, especially to Japan and Korea.

In the Song Dynasty, Chinese tea culture continued to develop, including the expansion of tea plantation and tea production, the high popularity of tea drinking, the prosperity of tea trade and tea-house and the highly developed literati tea culture. Unfortunately however, because of the Mongolian invasion and domination, Chinese tea culture almost ceased to develop in the Yuan Dynasty. This is reflected by the fact that, although there had been six treatises on tea in the Tang and the Five Dynasties and thirteen in the Song Dynasty, there was no such treatise in the Yuan Dynasty, and there were few tea activities like tea party, tea feast or tea competition in the Yuan Dynasty, which were very popular in the Tang and Song Dynasties, and there were much less tea drinking in life of populace. This declining tendency of Chinese tea culture did not reverse until the Ming Dynasty.

The Ming Dynasty took over Chinese tea culture from the hand of People, in fact, not Yuan people, but Song people and greatly developed it. With regard to cultivation techniques, people in the Ming Dynasty had carefully studied about suitable geographical and climate environment for tea growing and about the effects of earth, water, wind, rain, fog, sunshine on tea planting and tea picking. In respect of processing technique, by their diverse and more advanced methods people of the Ming Dynasty produced loose-leaf tea instead of tea cake which was the main form of tea product in the Tang and Song Dynasties, including green tea, scented tea, oolong tea, brown tea, white tea and black tea.

This means that the modern system of tea manufacture and tea products had been basically formed in the Ming Dynasty. As to drinking, they first made tea drink by a very particular process with certain fruits, nuts, grains and vegetables and had their drinking usually in a quiet and elegant environment.

Thus it can be seen that the modern Chinese tea culture had basically taken shape in the Ming Dynasty. And in the Qing Dynasty Chinese tea culture remained almost unchanged except that exportation of tea to the west was greatly increased and thereby a series of disputes, conflicts and wars were caused by it.

Modern Tea Culture

In modern China, virtually every dwelling—even down to the simplest mud hut—has a set of tea implements for brewing a cup of hot tea. They are symbols of welcome for visitors or neighbors. Traditionally, a visitor to a Chinese home is expected to sit down and drink tea while talking, visiting while remaining standing is considered uncouth. Folding the napkin in tea ceremonies is a traditional act in China performed to keep away bad qi energy. Tea ceremonies are held not only in daily life but also on important occasions.

A set of equipment for drinking tea

Tea was regarded as one of the seven daily necessities, the others being firewood, rice, oil, salt, soy sauce, and vinegar. There are several types of tea: green tea, oolong tea, red tea, black tea, white tea, yellow tea, Pu-erh tea and flower tea. Traditionally, fresh tea leaves are regularly turned over in a deep bowl. This process allows the leaves dry in a way that preserves their full flavor, ready for use.

Tea Drinking Customs

There are several special circumstances in which tea is prepared, consumed and preserved in Chinese culture.

To respect

According to Chinese tradition, members of the younger generation should show their respect to members of the older generation by offering a cup of tea. Inviting their elders to restaurants for tea is a traditional holiday activity. In the past, people of a lower social class served tea to the upper class in society. Today, with the increasing liberalization of Chinese society, this rule and its connotations have become blurred.

To apologize

In Chinese culture, tea may be offered as part of a formal apology. For example, children who have misbehaved may serve tea to their parents as a sign of regret and submission.

To show gratitude and celebrate weddings

In the traditional Chinese marriage ceremony, the bride and groom kneel in front of their respective parents and serve them tea and then thank them, together which represents an expre- ssion of their gratitude and respect. According to the tradition, the bride serves the groom's family, and the groom serves the bride's family. This process symbolizes the joining together of the two families.

Four Chinese tea cups

Light finger tapping is an informal way to thank the tea master or tea server for tea. While or after one's cup is filled, the receiver of the tea may tap the index and middle fingers (one or more in combination) to express gratitude to the person who served the tea. This custom is common in southern Chinese, where their meals often are accompanied by many servings of tea.

This custom was said to have originated in the Qing Dynasty when the Qianlong Emperor traveled in disguise throughout the empire and his accompanying servants were instructed not to reveal their master's identity. One day in a restaurant, the emperor poured tea for a servant. To that servant it was a huge honor to have the emperor pour him a cup of tea. Out of habit, he wanted to kneel and express his thanks to the emperor, but he could not do this since that would reveal the emperor's identity. Instead, he tapped the table with bent fingers to represent kneeling to the Emperor and to express his gratitude and respect. In this sense, the bent fingers supposedly signify a bowing servant. In formal tea ceremonies nodding the head or saying "thank you" is more appropriate.

Brewing Chinese Tea

The different ways of brewing Chinese tea depend on variables like the formality of the occasion, the means of the people preparing it, and the kind of tea being brewed. For example, green teas are more delicate than oolong teas or black teas, therefore, green tea should be brewed with cooler water. The most informal method of brewing tea is to simply add the leaves to a pot containing hot water. This method is commonly found in households and restaurants, for example, in the context of dim sum or yum cha in Cantonese restaurants. Another method for serving tea is to use a small lidded bowl called a gaiwan. The Hongwu Emperor of the Ming Dynasty contributed to the development of loose tea brewing by banning the production of compressed tea.

Influence on Chinese culture

Tea has a major influence on the development of Chinese culture, and Chinese traditional culture is closely connected with Chinese tea. Tea is often associated with literature, arts, and philosophy and is closely connected with Taoism, Buddhism and Confucianism. Roughly since the Tang Dynasty, drinking tea has been an essential part of self-cultivation. Chinese Chan (similar to Japanese Zen) philosophy is also linked with drinking tea.

A Yixing clay teapot

Teahouse

Ancient Chinese scholars used the teahouse as a place for sharing ideas. The teahouse was a place where political allegiances and social rank were said to have been temporarily suspended in favor of an honest and rational discourse. The leisurely consumption of tea promoted conviviality and civility amongst the participants. The teahouse is not only a minor by-product of Chinese tea culture, it offers historical evidence of Chinese tea history. Today, people can also sense a kind of humanistic atmosphere in Beijing's Lao She Teahouse and in other teahouses in East China cities like Hangzhou, Suzhou, Yangzhou, Nanjing, Wuxi, Shaoxing, Shanghai, and other places. The teahouse atmosphere is still dynamic and vigorous.

Words & Expressions

self-cultivation /ˈselfˌkʌltɪˈveɪʃən/ *n.* 修养，修身，自我修养，道德修养
fastidiousness /fæˈstɪdɪəsnəs/ *n.* 一丝不苟，严格
rituality /ˌrɪtjʊˈælətɪ/ *n.* 仪式
aulic /ˈɔːlɪk/ *adj.* 宫廷的
monograph /ˈmɒnəɡrɑːf/ *n.* 专题著作，专题论文；*vt.* 写关于…的专著
populace /ˈpɒpjələs/ *n.* 大众，平民，人口
recuperate /rɪˈkuːpəreɪt/ *vi.& vt.* 恢复，复原，挽回损失
eponymous /ɪˈpɒnɪməs/ *adj.* （书、戏剧等中的人物）与作品同名的，以…的名字命名的

set up *v.* 竖立；建立，装配，开业，

Notes

So monastic tea culture developed fast in the Tang Dynasty. Meanwhile, high quality of tea-leaves, luxury of tea sets, fastidiousness and rituality of tea drinking characterized the aulic tea culture.

因此，寺院茶文化在唐代发展迅速。同时，质量上乘的茶叶、奢华的茶具、一丝不苟的饮茶礼仪是宫廷茶文化的特点。

Reading Comprehension

I . Each piece of the following information is given in one of the paragraphs in the passage. Identify the paragraph from which the information is derived and put the corresponding number in the space provided.

(   ) 1. Before the 7th century BC, tea was known collectively under the term tu along with a great number of other bitter plants.

(　　) 2. Tea culture in China is different from that in European countries in preparation, taste, and occasion when it is consumed.

(　　) 3. Chinese youngsters should show their respect to the old by offering a cup of tea.

(　　) 4. That the bride and groom kneel in front of their respective parents and serve them tea symbolizes the joining together of the two families.

(　　) 5. The young who have misbehaved may serve tea to their parents as a sign of regret and submission.

Ⅱ. Decide whether the statements are true (T) or false (F) according to the passage.

(　　) 1. Light finger tapping is quite a formal way to appreciate the tea master or tea server for tea.

(　　) 2. The most informal method of brewing tea is to simply add the leaves to a pot containing hot water.

(　　) 3. Chinese traditional tea culture is closely connected with Chinese culture.

(　　) 4. Ancient Chinese scholars used the teahouse as a place for chatting.

(　　) 5. A set of tea is the symbol of welcome for visitors or neighbors.

Ⅲ. Discuss the following questions.

1. What are some special circumstances in which tea is prepared, consumed and preserved in Chinese tea culture?

2. Do you have the insights into the use of tea house by ancient Chinese scholars?

茶之美
Beauty of Tea

Tea Ceremony

The Gongfu tea ceremony or Gongfu tea ceremony, is a kind of Chinese tea ceremony, involving the ritual preparation and presentation of tea. It is probably based on the tea preparation approaches originated in Fujian and the Chaoshan area of eastern Guangdong. The term literally means "making tea with skill". Today, the approach is used popularly by teashops carrying tea of Chinese origins, and by tea connoisseurs as a way to maximize the taste of a tea selection, especially a finer one.

Attention to tea making quality has been a classic Chinese tradition. All teas, loose tea, coarse tea, and powdered tea have long coexisted with the "imperially appointed compressed form". By the end of the 14th century, the more naturalistic "loose leaf" form had become a popular household product and by the Ming era, loose tea was put to imperial use. In Japan, tea production began in the 12th century following Chinese models, and eventually evolved into the Japanese tea ceremony, meant to be exclusive to political and military elites. The related teaware that is the tea pot and later the gaiwan lidded cups were evolved. It is believed that the Gongfu tea preparation approach began only in around the 18th century. Some scholars think that it began in Wuyi in Fujian, where the production of oolong tea for export began; others believe that it was the people in Chaozhou in the Chaoshan area in Guangdong started this particular part of the tea culture. Senchado tea(日本煎茶) in Japan started in the early Edo period influenced from China.

Oral history from the 1940s still referred to Gongfu tea as "Chaoshan Gongfu cha". It is likely that regardless of the earliest incidence of the approach, the place that first successfully integrated it into daily life was Chaoshan area. Chaozhou is recognized by some as the "capital" of gongfu tea.

In essence, what is desired in Gongfu tea is a brew that tastes good and is satisfying to the soul. Tea masters in China and other Asian tea cultures study for years to perfect this method. However, method alone will not determine whether a great cup of tea will be produced. Essentially, two things have to be taken into consideration: chemistry and temperature.

Water chemistry

Water should be given careful consideration when conducting Gongfu tea. Water which tastes or smells bad will adversely affect the brewed tea. However, distilled or extremely soft water should never be used as this form of water lacks minerals, which will negatively affect the flavor of the tea and so can result in a "flat" brew. For these reasons, most tea masters will use a good clean local source of spring water. If this natural spring water is not available, bottled spring water will suffice. Yet high content mineral water also needs to be avoided. Hard water needs to be filtered.

Temperature

During the process of Gongfu tea, the tea master will first determine what is the appropriate temperature for the tea being used, in order to extract the aroma of the tea. An optimal temperature must be reached and maintained. The water temperature depends on the type of tea used. Guidelines are as follows: 75~85℃ for green tea (80℃ typical); 85~90℃ for white tea (90℃ typical); 95~100℃ for oolong tea; 100 ℃ (boiling) for compressed teas, such as pu-erh tea.

The temperature of the water can be determined by timing, as well as the size and the sizzling sound made by the air bubbles in the kettle.

At 75~85℃, the bubbles formed are known as "crab eyes" and are about 3mm in diameter. They are accompanied by loud, rapid sizzling sounds.

At 90~95℃, the bubbles, which are now around 8mm in diameter and accompanied by less frequent sizzling sounds and a lower sizzling pitch, are dubbed "fish eyes".

When the water is boiling, neither the formation of air bubbles nor sizzling sounds occurs. At high altitudes water boils at lower temperatures, so the above rules cannot be applied.

Tools and equipment

Below is a list of the main items used in a gongfu tea ceremony:

(1) Brewing vessel, Yixing teapot, porcelain teapot, or a covered bowl (gaiwan).

(2) Tea pitcher (chahai), or any matching size decanting vessel, used to ensure the consistency of the flavor of the tea (公道杯).

(3) Hot water kettle, e.g. an electric kettle.

(4) Brewing tray, or a deep, flat bottom porcelain plate to hold spills (spills are typical).

(5) Tea towel or tea cloth, usually dark colored.

(6) Tea knife or tea pick for clearing the teapot spout and separating leaves from tea cakes.

(7) Tea cups (traditionally 3 cups are used in most instances), matching size. Also named Pinming cup (品茗杯). Fragrance smelling cup is intended to capture the aroma and essence of the brewed tea, and is matched with the Pinming cups.

(8) Timer.

(9) Strainer, a tea strainer (漏斗) sometimes built into the tea pitchers.

(10) Tea holder, tea leaf holder for weighing and dispensing, or a wooden tea spoon to measure the amount of tea leaves required.

(11) Optional: tea basin or bowl used as the receptacle for used tea leaves and refuse water.

(12) Optional: scale.

(13) Optional: kitchen thermometer.

(14) Optional: scent cup (snifter cup) used to appreciate the tea's aroma (闻香杯).

(15) Optional: A pair of tongs called "jia" (挟) or "Giab" in both the Chaozhou and Minnan dialects.

(16) Optional: a calligraphy-style brush with a wooden handle, which is used to spread the wasted tea evenly over the tea tray to ensure no part dries out and the tea "stain" is spread evenly to ensure a pleasing colour to the tray.

(17) A tea pet, usually made from the same clay as a Yixing teapot, is fun to have. One kind of "tea pet" is a "tea boy." Prior to the tea ceremony, he is soaked in cold water. Hot water poured over him during the tea ceremony will make him "pee". Traditionally these 'pets' are classical Chinese figurines, such as a Dragon, Lion Turtle, or Toad, and are used as a receptacle over which the wasted tea is poured, usually to develop a patina.

Tea Set

A tea set or tea service is a collection of matching teaware and related utensils used in the preparation and serving of tea. The traditional components of a tea set may vary between societies and cultures.

Chinese style doll-sized tea set

The accepted history of the tea set began in China during the Han Dynasty. At this time, tea ware was made of porcelain and consisted of two styles: a northern white porcelain and a southern light blue porcelain. These ancient tea sets were not the creamer/sugar bowl companions that are now commonly used, but were rather bowls that would hold spiced or plain tea leaves, which would then have water poured over them. The bowls were multi-purpose, and used for a variety of cooking needs. In this period, tea was mainly used as a medicinal elixir, not as a daily drink for pleasure's sake.

It is believed the teapot was developed during the Song Dynasty. An archaeological dig turned up an ancient kiln that contained the remnants of a Yixing teapot. Yixing teapots, called zishahu in China and Redware Ceramic teapots in the U.S., are perhaps the most famous teapots. They are named for a tiny city located in Jiangsu Province, where a specific compound of iron ore results in the unique coloration of these teapots. They were fired without a glaze and were used to steep specific types of oolong teas. Because of the porous nature of the clay, the teapot would gradually be tempered by using it for brewing one kind of tea. This seasoning was part of the reason to use Yixing teapots. In addition, artisans created fanciful pots incorporating animal shapes.

The Song Dynasty also produced exquisite ceramic teapots and tea bowls in glowing glazes of brown, black and blue. A bamboo whisk was employed to beat the tea into a frothy confection highly prized by the Chinese.

A Chinese Yixing tea set used to serve guest contains the following items.

(1) A Yixing teapot.

(2) A tray to trap the wasted tea/water.

(3) Cups to drink the tea.

(4) A Tea tool kit which contains the following: digger, funnel, needle, shuffle, tongs and vase.

(5) A brush to wipe the wasted tea all over the tray to create an even tea stain.

(6) A Strainer—even if you pour tea from the pot, some tea leaf bits will still be poured out, so a sieve will help to filter out the loose bits during pouring.

(7) A clay animal or two. They are used for display and luck by many Chinese drinkers.

Teaware

Tea bowl (chawan) with hair fur's pattern, Jian ware from China during the Song Dynasty

Teaware (Table 6.2) is a broad international spectrum

of equipment used in the brewing and consumption of tea. Many components make up that spectrum, and vary greatly based upon the type of tea being prepared, and the cultural setting in which it is being prepared. This is often referred to as the tea ceremony, and holds much significance in many cultures, particularly in northwestern Europe and in eastern Asia.

Table 6.2　Teaware

	Teapot	Used to steep the tea leaves in hot water
	Teacup	Vessels from which to drink the hot tea out of which the leaves have been strained; there are many different kinds of tea cups
	Tea strainer	Used to extract leaves from tea solutions
	Tea tray	Used to keep the tea and hot water from spilling onto the table
	Tea ball and tea bag	Used to hold tea leaves in water for removal after steeping
	Tea caddy	For storing tea when not being consumed
	Tea cosy	A knitted cover for keeping a teapot hot after the tea is made

Tea equipment may be constructed of many materials, from iron in Japan to porcelain and clay in China, and also bamboo and other woods. Of particular repute are the Yixing clay teapots produced in eastern China.

Words & Expressions

connoisseur /ˌkɒnə'sɜː(r)/ *n.* 鉴赏家，内行
distilled /dɪ'stɪld/ *adj.* 由蒸馏得来的，净化的
suffice /sə'faɪs/ *v.* 足够，足以，满足…的需求，有能力
patina /'pætɪnə/ *n.* ［材］铜绿，光泽，神态，圣餐盘（复数 patinas 或 patinae）
evolve into 发展成，进化成

Notes

The 12 tea pieces for the elderly: 常见的 12 件茶具。
Song Dynasty teaware
1. Brazier (风炉)
2. Crushing block (砧椎)
3. Crushing roller (碾)
4. Stone mill (石磨)
5. Gourd scooper (瓢)
6. Sieve box (罗合)
7. Brush (札)
8. Bowl basket (畚)
9. Bowl (碗)
10. Water vessel (水方)
11. Tea whisk (茶筅)
12. Tea cloth (巾)

Reading Comprehension

I. Each piece of the following information is given in one of the paragraphs in the passage. Identify the paragraph from which the information is derived and put the corresponding number in the space provided.

(　　) 1. The production of oolong tea for export may begin from Fujian.
(　　) 2. By the end of the 14th century, the more naturalistic "loose leaf" form had become a popular household product.
(　　) 3. Gongfu tea ceremony literally means "making tea with skill".
(　　) 4. Distilled or extremely soft water should never be used for making tea as this form of water lacks minerals.
(　　) 5. Tea masters in China and other Asian tea cultures study for years to perfect this method.

II. Decide whether the statements are true (T) or false (F) according to the

passage.

(　　) 1. Extremely soft water will negatively affect the flavor of the tea, thus it should never be used for making tea.

(　　) 2. All teas, loose tea, coarse tea, and powdered tea have coexisted for short periods with the "imperially appointed compressed form".

(　　) 3. In gongfu tea ceremony, tea brewing tray is one of the main items.

(　　) 4. A tea pet is usually made of the different clay from tea pot.

(　　) 5. Gongfu tea ceremony is applied popularly by some teashops with tea of Chinese origins.

Development

III. Discuss the following questions.

1. What are the characteristics of gongfu tea ceremony?
2. Do you have more insights into the influence of Chinese tea ceremony?

第七章　蚕　桑

Chapter 7　Silkworm & Mulberry

蚕
Silkworm

  The silkworm is the larva or caterpillar of a silkmoth. It is an economically important insect, being a primary producer of silk. A silkworm's preferred food is white mulberry leaves, though they may eat other mulberry species and even *Osage* orange. Domestic silkmoths are closely dependent on humans for reproduction, as a result of millennia of selective breeding. Wild silkmoths are different from their domestic cousins as they have not been selectively bred; they are thus not as commercially viable in the production of silk.

  Sericulture, the practice of breeding silkworms for the production of raw silk, has been under way for at least 5000 years in China, whence it spread to India, Korea, Japan, and the West. The domestic silkmoth was domesticated from the wild silkmoth *Bombyx mandarina*, which has a range from northern India to northern China, Korea, Japan, and the far eastern regions of Russia. The domestic silkmoth derives from Chinese rather than Japanese or Korean stock.

  Silkmoths were unlikely to have been domestically bred before the Neolithic Age. Before then, the tools to manufacture quantities of silk thread had not been developed. The domesticated B. mori and the wild B. mandarina can still breed and sometimes produce hybrids. Domestic silkmoths are very different from most members in the genus *Bombyx*; not only have they lost the ability to fly, but their color pigments have also been lost.

  Mulberry silkworms can be categorized into three different but connected groups or types. The major groups of silkworms fall under the univoltine ("uni-"=one, "voltine"= brood frequency) and bivoltine categories. The univoltine type is generally linked with the geographical area within greater Europe. The eggs of this type hibernate during winter due to the cold climate, and cross-fertilize only by spring, generating silk only once annually. The second type is called bivoltine and is normally found in China, Japan and Korea. The breeding process of this type takes place twice annually, a feat made possible through the slightly warmer climates and the resulting two life cycles. The polyvoltine type of mulberry silkworm can only be found in the tropics. The eggs are laid by female moths and hatch within nine to 12 days, so the resulting type can have up to eight separate life cycles throughout the year.

Eggs take about 14 days to hatch into larvae, which eat continuously. They have a preference for white mulberry, having an attraction to the mulberry odorant *cis*-jasmone. They are not monophagous, since they can eat other species of Morus, as well as some other Moraceae, mostly Osage orange. They are covered with tiny black hairs. When the color of their heads turns darker, it indicates they are about to molt. After molting, the larval phase of the silkworms emerge white, naked, and with little horns on their backs.

After they have molted four times, their bodies become slightly yellow, and the skin becomes tighter. The larvae then prepare to enter the pupal phase of their life cycle, and enclose themselves in a cocoon made up of raw silk produced by the salivary glands. The final molt from larva to pupa takes place within the cocoon, which provides a vital layer of protection during the vulnerable, almost motionless pupal state. Many other Lepidoptera produce cocoons, but only a few—the Bombycidae, in particular the genus *Bombyx*, and the Saturniidae, in particular the genus *Antheraea*—have been exploited for fabric production.

If the animal is allowed to survive after spinning its cocoon and through the pupal phase of its life cycle, it releases proteolytic enzymes to make a hole in the cocoon so it can emerge as an adult moth. These enzymes are destructive to the silk and can cause the silk fibers to break down from over a mile in length to segments of random length, which seriously reduces the value of the silk threads, but not silk cocoons used as "stuffing" available in China and elsewhere for doonas, jackets, etc. To prevent this, silkworm cocoons are boiled. The heat kills the silkworms and the water makes the cocoons easier to unravel. Often, the silkworm itself is eaten.

As the process of harvesting the silk from the cocoon kills the larva, sericulture has been criticized by animal welfare and rights activists. Mahatma Gandhi was critical of silk production based on the Ahimsa philosophy "not to hurt any living thing". This led to Gandhi's promotion of cotton spinning machines, an example of which can be seen at the Gandhi Institute. He also promoted Ahimsa silk, wild silk made from the cocoons of wild and semiwild silkmoths.

The moth—the adult phase of the life cycle—is not capable of functional flight, in contrast to the wild *B. mandarina* and other *Bombyx* species, whose males fly to meet females and for evasion from predators. Some may emerge with the ability to lift off and stay airborne, but sustained flight cannot be achieved. This is because their bodies are too big and heavy for their small wings. However, some silkmoths can still fly. Silkmoths have a wing span of 3~5cm (1.2~2.0in) and a white, hairy body. Females are about two to three times bulkier than males (for they are carrying many eggs), but are similarly colored. Adult Bombycidae have reduced mouth parts and do not feed, though a human caretaker can feed them.

Domestication of Silkworm

The domestic species of silkworm, compared to the wild species, has increased cocoon size, body size, growth rate, and efficiency of its digestion. It has gained tolerance to human presence and handling, and also to living in crowded conditions. The male domestic silkmoth cannot fly, so it needs human assistance in finding a mate, and it lacks fear of potential predators. The native color pigments have also been lost, so the domestic silkmoths are leucistic, since camouflage is not useful when they only live in captivity. These changes have made the domesticated strains entirely dependent upon humans for survival. The eggs are kept in incubators to aid in their hatching.

Silkworm breeding

Silkworms were first domesticated in China over 5000 years ago. Since then, the silk production capacity of the species has increased nearly tenfold. The silkworm is one of the few organisms wherein the principles of genetics and breeding were applied to harvest maximum output. It is second only to maize in exploiting the principles of heterosis and crossbreeding.

Silkworm breeding is aimed at the overall improvement of silkworms from a commercial point of view. The major objectives are improving fecundity (the egg-laying capacity of a breed), the health of larvae, quantity of cocoon and silk production, and disease resistance. Healthy larvae lead to a healthy cocoon crop. Health is dependent on factors such as better pupation rate, fewer dead larvae in the mountage, shorter larval duration (this lessens the chance of infection) and bluish-tinged fifth-instar larvae (which are healthier than the reddish-brown ones). Quantity of cocoon and production of silk are directly related to the pupation rate and larval weight. Healthier larvae have greater pupation rates and cocoon weights. Quality of cocoon and silk depends on a number of factors, including genetics.

Hobby raising and school projects

The domestic silkmoth has been raised as a hobby in countries such as China, South Africa, Zimbabwe and Iran. Children often pass on the eggs, creating a non-commercial population. The experience provides children with the opportunity to witness the life cycle of silkmoths. The practice of raising silkmoths by children as pets has, in non-silk farming South Africa, led to the development of extremely hardy landraces of silkmoths, because they are invariably subjected to hardships not encountered by commercially farmed members of the species. However, these worms, not being selectively bred as such, are possibly inferior in silk production and may exhibit other undesirable traits.

Genome

The full genome of the domestic silkmoth was published in 2008 by the International Silkworm Genome Consortium. Draft sequences were published in 2004. The genome of the domestic silkmoth is mid-range with a genome size around 432 megabase pairs.

High genetic variability has been found in domestic lines of silkmoths, though this is less than that among wild silkmoths (about 83% of wild genetic variation). This suggests a single event of domestication, and that it happened over a short period of time, with a large number of wild silkworms having been collected for domestication. Major questions, however, remain unanswered: "Whether this event was in a single location or in a short period of time in several locations cannot be deciphered from the data". Research also has yet to identify the area in China where domestication arose.

Sericulture

Sericulture, or silk farming, is the cultivation of silkworms to produce silk. Although there are several commercial species of silkworms, *Bombyx mori* (the caterpillar of the domesticated silk moth) is the most widely used and intensively studied silkworm. Silk was first produced in China as early as the Neolithic period. Sericulture has become an important cottage industry in countries such as Brazil, China, France, India, Italy, Japan, Korea and Russia. Today, China and India are the two main producers, with more than 60% of the world's annual production.

According to Confucian text, the discovery of silk production dates to about 2700 BC, although archaeological records point to silk cultivation as early as the Yangshao period (5000 BC—3000 BC). By about the first half of the 1st century AD it had reached ancient Khotan, by a series of interactions along the Silk Road. By 140 AD the practice had been established in India. In the 6th century the smuggling of silkworm eggs into the Byzantine Empire led to its establishment in the Mediterranean, remaining a monopoly in the Byzantine Empire for centuries(Byzantine silk). In 1147 AD, during the Second Crusade, Roger II of Sicily (1095—1154) attacked Corinth and Thebes, two important centres of Byzantine silk production, capturing the weavers and their equipment and establishing his own silk works in Palermo and Calabria, eventually spreading the industry to Western Europe.

Silkworm larvae are fed with mulberry leaves and after the fourth moult, they climb a twig placed near them and spin their silken cocoons. This process is achieved by the worm through a dense fluid secreted from its structural glands, resulting in the fibre of the cocoon. The silk is a continuous filament comprising fibroin protein, secreted from two salivary glands in the head of each larva, and a gum called sericin, which cements the filaments. The sericin is removed by placing the cocoons in hot water, which frees the silk filaments and readies them for reeling. This is known as the degumming process. The immersion in hot water also kills the silkworm pupa. Single filaments are combined to form thread, which is drawn under tension through several guides and wound onto reels.

The threads may be plied to form yarn. After drying, the raw silk is packed according to quality.

The stages of production are as follows:

(1) The silk moth lays thousands of eggs.

(2) The silk moth eggs hatch to form larvae or caterpillars, known as silkworms.

(3) The larvae feed on mulberry leaves.

(4) Having grown and moulted several times, the silkworm weaves a net to hold itself.

(5) It swings its head from side to side in a figure "8" distributing the saliva that will form silk.

(6) The silk solidifies when it contacts the air.

(7) The silkworm spins approximately one mile of filament and completely encloses itself in a cocoon in about two or three days. The amount of usable quality silk in each cocoon is small. As a result, about 2500 silkworms are required to produce a pound of raw silk.

(8) The intact cocoons are boiled, killing the silkworm pupa.

(9) The silk is obtained by brushing the undamaged cocoon to find the outside end of the filament.

(10) The silk filaments are then wound on a reel. One cocoon contains approximately 1000 yards of silk filament. The silk at this stage is known as raw silk. One thread comprises up to 48 individual silk filaments.

Words & Expressions

larva /ˈlɑːrvə/ n. 幼虫；幼体
silkmoth /ˈsɪlk mɒθ/ n. 蚕蛾
sericulture /ˈserɪˌkʌltʃər/ n. 养蚕，蚕丝业
molt /məʊlt/ vi. & vt. 脱毛，换毛；n. 换毛，脱皮，换毛期
cocoon /kəˈkuːn/ n. 茧，卵囊
Bombyx mandarina /ˈbɑːnbɪks/ /ˈmændərɪnə/ n. 野桑蚕
leucistic /luːˈkɪstɪk/ adj. [动] 白毛的，先天性色素缺乏的
camouflage /ˈkæməflɑːʒ/ n. & vt. & vi. 伪装，掩饰
maize /meɪz/ n. 玉米
heterosis /ˌhetəˈrəʊsɪs/ n. 杂种优势
pupae /ˈpjuːpiː/ n. 蛹（pupa 的复数形式）
genome /ˈdʒiːnəʊm/ n. 基因组，染色体组

Notes

After they have molted four times, their bodies become slightly yellow, and the skin becomes tighter. The larvae then prepare to enter the pupal phase of their life cycle, and enclose themselves in a cocoon made up of raw silk produced by the salivary glands. The final molt from larva to pupa takes place within the cocoon, which provides a vital layer of protection during the vulnerable, almost motionless pupal state.

蚕蜕皮四次后，身体变浅黄色，皮肤变得更紧。然后，幼虫准备进入其生命周期的蛹阶段，并将自己包裹在一个由唾液腺产生的生丝组成的茧中。从幼虫到蛹的最后一次蜕皮发生在茧内，这为脆弱的、几乎静止的蛹提供了一层至关重要的保护。

The moth—the adult phase of the life cycle—is not capable of functional flight, in contrast to the wild *B. mandarina* and other *Bombyx* species, whose males fly to meet females and for evasion from predators.

飞蛾是生命周期的成年阶段，它没有功能性的飞行能力，相比之下，野生野嘴蛾和其他家蛾的雄性可以飞并能遇到雌性，可躲避捕食者。

Reading Comprehension

I. Each piece of the following information is given in one of the paragraphs in the passage. Identify the paragraph from which the information is derived and put the corresponding number in the space provided.

(　　) 1. Silkworm is an economically important insect, being a primary producer of silk.

(　　) 2. Larvae have a preference for white mulberry, having an attraction to the mulberry odorant *cis*-jasmone.

(　　) 3. The univoltine type of mulberry silkworm is generally connected with the geographical regions within greater Europe.

(　　) 4. Before Neolithic Age, the tools to manufacture the silk thread had not been developed.

(　　) 5. The final molt from larva to pupa takes place within the cocoon.

(　　) 6. Sericulture is the practice of breeding silkworms for the production of raw silk and has been in China for at least 5000 years.

II. Decide whether the statements are true (T) or false (F) according to the passage.

(　　) 1. Because the heat kills the silkworms and the water makes the cocoons easier to unravel, silkworm cocoons are boiled and the silkworm itself is eaten.

(　　) 2. Adult Bombycidae have increased mouth parts and do not feed, though a human caretaker can feed them.

(　　) 3. Domestic silkmoths are closely separated from humans for reproduction, because of millennia of selective breeding.

(　　) 4. Some moth may emerge with the ability to lift off and stay airborne, but sustained flight cannot be achieved.

(　　) 5. The domestic silkmoth derives from Chinese rather than Japanese or Korean stock.

Language Focus

III. Complete the sentences with the correct form of the words in the table.

airborne	cocoon	unravel	spin	wing
caretaker	feed	functional	enzyme	phase

1. She saw the occasional glimmer of a moth's _____.
2. Many people are allergic to _____ pollutants such as pollen.
3. They put their chairs on their desks so that the _____ could sweep the floor.
4. They knew absolutely nothing about handling or _____ a baby.
5. A _____ is a covering of silky threads that the larvae of moths and other insects make for themselves before they grow into adults.
6. Most kids will go through a _____ of being faddy about what they eat.
7. He was good with his hands and could _____ a knot or untangle yarn that others wouldn't even attempt.
8. We have fully _____ smoke alarms on all staircases.
9. This _____ would make the filtration of beer easier.
10. Michelle will also _____ a customer's wool fleece to specification at a cost of $2.25 an ounce.

IV. Match the sentences in Section A with the English translation in Section B.

Section A

1. 家蚕是从野生蚕蛾驯养而来的，遍布于从印度北部到中国北部、韩国、日本和俄罗斯远东地区。
2. 桑蚕可分为三种不同但相互联系的类群或类型。
3. 因为野生蚕蛾没有经选择性地饲养，所以它们与其他的驯养亲属不同。
4. 蛾在成虫阶段不能进行飞行。
5. 多伏坦型桑蚕只在热带地区生存。

Section B

1. Mulberry silkworms can be categorized into three different but connected groups or types.
2. Wild silkmoths are different from their domestic cousins as they have not been selectively bred.
3. The domestic silkmoth was domesticated from the wild silkmoth *Bombyx mandarina*, which has a range from northern India to northern China, Korea, Japan and the far eastern regions of Russia.
4. The polyvoltine type of mulberry silkworm can only be found in the tropics.
5. The moth—the adult phase of the life cycle—is not capable of functional flight.

V. Translate the paragraph into Chinese.

Bombyx mori, the domestic silkmoth, is an insect from the moth family Bombycidae.

It is the closest relative of *Bombyx mandarina*, the wild silkmoth. The silkworm is the larva or caterpillar of a silkmoth. It is an economically important insect, being a primary producer of silk. A silkworm's preferred food is white mulberry leaves, though they may eat other mulberry species. Domestic silkmoths are closely dependent on humans for reproduction, as a result of millennia of selective breeding.

VI. Discuss the following questions.
1. What are the characteristics of silkworm?
2. What are the differences between wild silkworm and domesticated silkworm?

Text B 桑 Mulberry

Mulberry or called *Morus*, a genus of flowering plants in the family Moraceae, comprises 10~16 species of deciduous trees commonly known as mulberries, growing wild and under cultivation in many temperate world regions.

Mulberries are fast-growing when young, but soon become slow-growing and rarely exceed 10~15m (30~50ft) tall. The leaves are alternately arranged, simple, and often lobed and serrated on the margin. Lobes are more common on juvenile shoots than on mature trees. The trees can be monoecious or dioecious. The mulberry fruit is a multiple fruit, about 2~3cm long. Immature fruits are white, green, or pale yellow. In most species, the fruit turn pink and then red while ripening, then dark purple or black, and have a sweet flavor when fully ripe. The fruit of the white-fruited cultivar are white when ripe; the fruit of this cultivar are also sweet, but have a mild flavor compared with darker varieties. Although quite similar looking, they are not to be confused with blackberries.

Mulberries can be grown from seed, and this is often advised, as seedling-grown trees are generally of better shape and health, but they are most often planted from large cuttings, which root readily. The mulberry plants allowed to grow tall have a crown height of 1.5~1.8m (5~6ft) from ground level and a stem girth of 10~13cm (4~5in). They are specially raised with the help of well-grown saplings 8~10 months old of any of the varieties recommended for rain-fed areas like S-13 (for red loamy soil) or S-34 (black cotton soil), which are tolerant to drought or soil-moisture stress conditions. Usually, the plantation is raised and in block formation with a spacing of 1.8 by 1.8m (6 by 6ft), or 2.4 by 2.4m (8 by 8ft), as plant-to-plant and row-to-row distances. The plants are usually pruned once a year during the monsoon season to a height of 1.5~1.8m (5~6ft) and allowed to grow with a maximum of 8~10 shoots at the crown. The leaves are harvested three or four times a year by a leaf-picking method under rain-fed or semiarid conditions, depending on the monsoon. The tree branches pruned during the fall season (after the leaves have fallen) are cut and used to make durable baskets supporting agriculture and animal husbandry. Only the male mulberry trees produce pollen, this lightweight pollen can be inhaled deeply into the lungs, sometimes triggering asthma. Conversely, female mulberry trees produce all-female flowers, which draw pollen and dust from the air. Because of this pollen-absorbing feature, all-female mulberry trees have an OPALS allergy scale rating of just 1 (lowest level of allergy potential), and some consider it "allergy-free".

Mulberry tree scion wood can easily be grafted onto other mulberry trees during the winter, when the tree is dormant. One common scenario is converting a problematic male mulberry tree to an allergy-free female tree, by grafting all-female mulberry tree scions to a male mulberry that has been pruned back to the trunk. However, any new growth from below the graft(s) must be removed, as they would be from the original male mulberry tree.

The fruit of the white mulberry—an East Asian species extensively naturalized in urban regions of eastern North America—has a different flavor, sometimes characterized as refreshing and a little tart, with a bit of gumminess to it and a hint of vanilla. In North America, the white mulberry is considered an invasive exotic and has taken over extensive tracts from native plant species, including the red mulberry.

The ripe fruit is edible and is widely used in pies, tarts, wines, cordials, and herbal teas. The fruit of the black mulberry (native to southwest Asia) and the red mulberry (native to eastern North America) have the strongest flavors, which have been likened to "fireworks in the mouth".

The fruit and leaves are sold in various forms as nutritional supplements. The mature plant contains significant amounts of resveratrol, particularly in stem bark. Unripe fruit and green parts of the plant have a white sap that may be toxic, stimulating, or mildly hallucinogenic.

Mulberry leaves, particularly those of the white mulberry, are ecologically important as the sole food source of the silkworm (*Bombyx mori*, named after the mulberry genus *Morus*), the cocoon of which is used to make silk. The wild silk moth also eats mulberry. Other Lepidoptera larvae—which include the common emerald, lime hawk-moth, sycamore moth, and fall webworm—also eat the plant.

Mulberry fruit color derives from anthocyanins, which are under basic research for mechanisms of various diseases. Anthocyanins are responsible for the attractive colors of fresh plant foods, including orange, red, purple, black, and blue. These colors are water-soluble and easily extractable, yielding natural food colorants. Due to a growing demand for natural food colorants, their significance in the food industry is increasing.

A cheap and industrially feasible method has been developed to extract anthocyanins from mulberry fruit that could be used as a fabric dye or food colorant of high color value (above 100). Scientists found that, of 31 Chinese mulberry cultivars tested, the total anthocyanin yield varied from 148 to 2725mg/L of fruit juice. All the sugars, acids and vitamins of the fruit remained intact in the residual juice after removal of the anthocyanins, so the juice could be used to produce juice, wine and sauce.

Anthocyanin content depends on climate and area of cultivation, and is particularly high in sunny climates. This finding holds promise for tropical countries that grow mulberry trees as part of the practice of sericulture to profit from industrial anthocyanin production through the recovery of anthocyanins from the mulberry fruit.

Cultivation of Mulberry

Mulberry can grow practically on any type of land except on very steep lands. Good growths, however, are obtained when it is raised on either flat land or gently sloping or undulating lands. On more sloppy or steep lands, necessary attention to proper soil conservation methods as contour drains, contour planting or even bench terracing should be given.

Mulberry cultivation can be done in a wide range of soils, but best growth is obtained in loamy to clayey loam soils. The mulberry plant can tolerate slightly acidic conditions in the soil. In the case of too acidic soils with pH below 5, necessary corrective measures through application of dolomite or lime should be adopted. In the case of alkaline soils, application of gypsum should be resorted to correction of the soil alkalinity.

Since mulberry is a deep-rooted plant, the soil should be sufficiently deep up to about two feet in depth. In respect of elevation, mulberry thrives well up to about 4000 feet, above growth will be retarded because of the cooler temperature.

Land preparation for mulberry plantation

Mulberry falls under the category of perennial crops and once it is properly raised during the first year, it can come to full yielding capacity during the second year and lasts for over 15 years in the field without any significant deterioration in the yield of the leaf. Usually, flat lands are suitable for irrigated mulberry cultivation. If the slope is more than 15%, suitable land development measures such as contour bunding, bench terracing, etc. should be adopted.

In mulberry cultivation, the field should be prepared by deep plowing up to a depth of 30~45cm in order to loosen the soil and thereafter with a country plow or tractor to bring the soil to a fine tilth. Weeds, stones should be removed during the preparatory stage. A basal dose of farmyard manure 20 tonnes per hectare is recommended, which has to be thoroughly incorporated into the soil. Farmlands along the highways, in the vicinity of factories, area irrigated by raw sewage and untreated effluents, plots abetting other gardens with intensive pesticide usage, waterlogged areas and tobacco grown land are not suitable locations for mulberry cultivation.

Selection of variety for mulberry production

The criteria for selection of variety includes fertility of the land, water availability, region specificity, the extent of the garden and problematic soils. The yield potential of high yielding varieties can be best realized in high fertility soils and they respond to intensive irrigation. Wherever the size of the operation is bigger, it is advisable to have a separate garden for chawki rearing for which a variety can be chosen in addition to a high yielding variety for rearing late age worms. In alkaline soils, the variety AR-12 is suitable. An improved selection is a superior variety evolved by the institute, which is a vigorous strain responding well to manuring and capable of giving about 25% more leaf yield. This variety thrives well both under dry as well as irrigated conditions. Quality wise also, it is superior to the local variety of mulberry and, therefore, could be used with great advantage in mulberry cultivation.

Planting material and plantation of mulberry

Plantation in mulberry cultivation can be taken up both by cuttings and saplings. However, saplings are always better than cuttings as planting material for quick and better establishment. Two cuttings or one sapling are planted at each spot in desired spacing, Cuttings are planted keeping one bud exposed while the saplings are planted in pits opened at the spot.

Preparation of cuttings in mulberry farming

Cuttings should be prepared from well-matured 6~8 months old shoots of about 1.5cm in diameter. Cuttings of 15~20cm length with 3~4 healthy buds are selected for plantation.

Raising of saplings for mulberry plantation

Nursery beds with a dimension of 5m×1.5m are prepared. The land is dug to a depth of 30~40cm and the soil should be pulverized well. FYM is applied at 15kg per bed and mixed well with the soil. Some quantity of sand is also added to heavy (clayey) soils to make the soil loose and friable, while some quantity of tank silt or other well decomposed organic matter has to be applied to sandy soils to increase the water holding capacity.

Nursery beds with a spacing of 15cm×10cm. The full length of cutting is pushed into the soil keeping only one bud exposed above the ground. It should be irrigated twice a week. Fertilizer is applied at 25 : 25 : 25 (N : P : K) kg per hectare after 5~6 weeks when plants sprout well and the root system is established. In mulberry cultivation, saplings of about 80~90 days old can be used for planting. While uprooting the saplings, maximum care should be taken to avoid damage to the root system.

In mulberry cultivation, spacing depends upon the soil conditions, slope, variety and convenience for inter-cultural operations. In the case of rainfed mulberry gardens, the aim should be to raise the mulberry plant with a sturdier frame so that it is able to withstand prevailing drought conditions.

Planting of mulberry

Pit system is ideal in 90cm×90cm spacing. Pits of 35cm^3 are dug and left for one month, which is later filled with FYM and soil at 1 : 2 ratio. Trenches of 35cm×35cm are also convenient to take up plantation in mulberry cultivation. It is preferable to start the plantation during the rainy season. In hilly areas, 3 cuttings of 20~22cm length are planted in each pit at a spacing of 15cm. Cuttings not sprouting in 4~5 weeks need to be replaced by saplings to ensure the required plant density.

Manuring and fertilizers of mulberry plant

Application of a basal dose of organic manure like compost or cattle manure is necessary for the successful establishment of the garden. Thereafter, the young growing plants should be assisted to put forth vigorous and maximum growth through periodical fertilizer applications.

FYM has to be applied about 20t/ha/year in two doses following the first bottom pruning and third pruning. Fertilizers have to be applied as per the recommended schedule and secondary and micronutrients have to be applied wherever necessary. Foliar sprays such as boron (1%), urea (0.5%), zinc sulphate (0.1%), etc. will improve the leaf quality.

Harvesting of mulberry leaves

Picking of leaves should be carried out in time in mulberry cultivation, that is to say when the leaves are at the correct stage of maturity for harvest. Otherwise, part of the leaves will become over mature coarse and suffer in quality from the point of view of nutritive value for the silkworms. Also part of the leaves may turn yellow, shed and be lost. Therefore, timely harvest, as the leaves reach the required stage of maturity, will lead to a fuller harvest of the available leaves without wastage, and realization of maximum yield.

Yield in mulberry cultivation

Normally the expected annual yield is 40~50t of leaves per acre. In shoot harvest method, harvesting can be done at an interval of 70 days (5 harvests). In case of leaf harvest method, the first harvest is taken 70 days after 1st pruning and 2nd and 3rd harvest (coinciding with 2nd bottom pruning) at an interval of 55 days. The fourth harvest is taken 70 days after the 3rd harvest and 5th and 6th at an interval of 55 days.

Construction of rearing shelter for silkworms

Mulberry silkworm rearing, being completely domesticated, demands specified environmental conditions like optimum temperature (24~28℃) and relative humidity (70%~85%). It is, therefore, necessary to evolve measures for economic cooling through a selection of proper material for wall and roof fabrication, the orientation of the building, using the right construction method/design, etc. Further, enough space must be available to carry out leaf preservation, chawki rearing, late age rearing, and molting and also its effective cleaning and disinfection.

The size of the silkworm rearing house depends upon the quantum and type of rearing. The different types of rearing are shelf or stand rearing, platform rearing, and floor rearing. Shelf rearing requires minimum space and is most common in India. A floor area of 150 sft.

can provide rearing space for 100 crossbred(CB) DFLs or 75 bivoltine(BV) DFLs.

In platform rearing, the larvae are shifted to shoot rearing platforms after a 3rd molt. The ideal size of each platform will be 5ft×25ft. which can accommodate 50 DFLs up to the stage of spinning. Platforms can be arranged in two/ three tiers with a gap of 2~3ft. A building floor area of 250~300sft. is required to rear 100 DFLs of CB layings or 75 DFLs of BV layings.

Cultural Symbols of Mulberry

The mulberry tree has come to represent different ideas among different cultures. It has been the sign of nature, faith, growth and for some death. The mulberry tree thrives in Asia, Europe and the Middle East. Its berries are edible, its supple wood is good for carving and its bark and leaves are used to make paper. So prominent are the uses and attributes of the mulberry tree that, in all of these places, this plant became wrapped in legends, history and meaning.

Attributes

Mulberries do not bud until all danger of frost is past, and so they symbolize calculated patience. When they do produce buds, it happens so quickly that it seems to occur overnight, displaying and thus symbolizing expediency and wisdom. For all these attributes, the ancient Greeks dedicated the plant to the goddess of wisdom, Athena (a.k.a. the Roman goddess Minerva).

Chinese symbolism

The sun in Chinese legend is represented by the three-legged Sun Bird. This bird resides in the eastern sea, atop a magnificent mulberry tree. This tree is said to be the link between earth and the eastern heaven. Depictions of mulberry trees in art are often symbols of this divine tree. The mulberry is also a symbol of the archer because legend tells how the first bow was made by Emperor Huangdi to defeat a tiger who had chased him into a mulberry tree.

Japanese symbolism

Mulberry paper is used as vessels for offerings in Shinto shrines. Japanese families often used mulberries as a part of their family crests, and strips of the fiber were hung from sacred trees as prayers. The mulberry leaves were also used to feed silk worms, who produced the fiber to make kimonos fit for the ruling class. In all of these capacities, the mulberry represents support, nurturing and self-sacrifice.

Greek symbolism

The mulberry tree is featured in the works of Ovid and in Shakespeare's *A Midsummer Night's Dream* in the tale of Pyramus and Thisbe. These two young lovers were forbidden to wed, so they arranged to meet secretly under a mulberry tree. They both perished under the tree, and their blood is said to have stained the white berries dark red. To this day, the red berries of the mulberry tree carry the symbolism of star-crossed lovers and of the final union of death.

History

The well-renowned author of *Paradise Lost*, John Milton, was said to have planted a mulberry tree at Cambridge and at Stowmarket, these trees are still thriving today. Shakespeare planted a tree at Stratford-on-Avon, which supposedly came from the mulberry garden of James Ⅰ. Though this tree was chopped down, a few cuttings of it were transplanted at various spots around England, and the wood from this tree was fashioned into countless mementos of the poet and playwright. These mulberry trees are now symbolic of those famous British writers.

Words

genus /'dʒiːnəs/ *n.* 类，种，属
Moraceae /'mɔːrəsi,iː/ *n.* 桑科
deciduous /dɪ'sɪdʒuəs/ *adj.* 落叶性的，脱落性的，非永久性的
monoecious /mɒ'niːʃəs/ *adj.* 雌雄同株的；雄雌同体的
graft /grɑːft/ *n. & v.* 嫁接，移植
gumminess /ɡʌmɪnɪs/ *n.* 黏性，树胶质
hallucinogenic /həˌluːsɪnə'dʒenɪk/ *adj.* 引起幻觉的，迷幻药的

Notes

Mulberry or called *Morus*, a genus of flowering plants in the family Moraceae, comprises 10~16 species of deciduous trees commonly known as mulberries, growing wild and under cultivation in many temperate world regions.

桑或称为桑树，是桑树科开花植物的一个属，包括 10~16 种落叶树，通常被称为桑，在许多温带地区野生和种植。

Reading Comprehension

Ⅰ. **Each piece of the following information is given in one of the paragraphs in the passage. Identify the paragraph from which the information is derived and put the corresponding number in the space provided.**

(   ) 1. Mulberry tree branches pruned during the fall season, after the leaves have fallen, are cut and used to make durable baskets supporting agriculture and animal husbandry.

(   ) 2. Mulberry leaves are simple and often lobed and serrated on the margin.

(   ) 3. Mulberries grow wild and under cultivation in many temperate world regions.

(   ) 4. The fruit of the white mulberry with a different flavor is characterized as refreshing.

(   ) 5. The fruit of the black mulberry and the red mulberry have the strongest flavors.

(   ) 6. Mulberry tree scion wood can easily be grafted onto other mulberry trees during the winter.

II. Decide whether the statements are true (T) or false (F) according to the passage.

(   ) 1. Mulberry fruit and leaves are exported in various forms as nutritional supplements.

(   ) 2. Calcium of 39mg per 100g is contained in raw mulberry.

(   ) 3. Vitamin C is rich in raw mulberries.

(   ) 4. Mulberry leaves are not the most important as the food source of the silkworm.

(   ) 5. Immature mulberry fruits are pink, green, or pale yellow.

III. Discuss the following questions.

1. What are the features of mulberry?

2. Do you have more insights into the nutrition of mulberry fruit according to Chinese medicine?

Text C 蚕桑文化 Culture of Silkworm and Mulberry

The culture of silkworm and mulberry has been developped well along the silk Road. The Silk Road was a network of trade routes connecting the East and the West in ancient and Medieval times. The term is used for both overland routes and those that are marine or limnic. The Silk Road is named after the lucrative international trade in Chinese silk textiles that started during the Han dynasty. Using one single name for this intricate web of trade routes is a modern invention; the name Silk Road was coined by the geographer Ferdinand Von Richthofen in the late 19th century. Unsurprisingly, use of the term Silk Road is not uncontroversial.

The Silk Road involved three continents: Europe, Africa and Asia.

Main Routes of the Silk Road

In addition to silk, a wide range of other goods was traded along the Silk Road, and the network was also important for migrants and travellers, and for the spread of religion, philosophy, science, technology, and artistic ideals. The Silk Road had a significant impact on the lands through which the routes passed, and the trade played a significant role in the development of towns and cities along the Silk Road routes.

Many merchants along the Silk Road were involved in relay trade, where an item would change owners many times and travel a little bit with each one of them before reaching its final buyer. It seems to have been highly unusual for any individual merchant to travel all the way between China and Europe or Northern Africa. Instead, various merchants specialized in transporting goods through various sections of the Silk Road.

Examples of goods traded along the Silk Road:
- Silk textiles, lacquer-ware and porcelain from China.
- Sandalwood from India.
- Saffron, pistachio nuts and dates from Persia.
- Myrrh and frankincense from Somalia.
- Glass bottles from Egypt.

Overland Routes

The Silk Road consisted of several routes. Among the overland routes, the dominating ones were the Northern route, the Southern route and the Southwestern route.

The Northern Route

The easternmost point of the northern route was Chang'an, an important city in central China. Chang'an was the capital for more than ten different Chinese dynasties.

The northern route became popular around the first century BC, when the Chinese Emperor Wu of Han, who reigned from 141 to 87 BC, used his army to keep nomadic tribes from attacking travellers within his sphere of influence.

From Chang'an, the northern route went northwest through the Chinese provinces Shaanxi and Gansu, before splitting into three different routes.
- #1 followed the mountain ranges north of the Taklamakan Desert.
- #2 followed the mountain ranges south of the Taklamakan Desert.
- #3 went north of the Tian Shan mountains through Turpan, Talgar and Almaty in what is now southeastern Kazakhstan.

#1 and #2 rejoined each other again at Kashgar, an oasis city in today's Xinjiang. After Kashgar, the routes split again, with a southern branch going down towards Termez and Balkh, and a northern branch going to Kokand and then west across the Karakum Desert.

Before reaching Merv in Turkmenistan, both routes joined the main southern route.

One branch of the northern route turned off to the northwest instead of continuing westwards. This one past the Aral Sea and went north of the Caspian Sea, before reaching the Black Sea.

The Southern Route

The southern route went from China through the Karakoram mountains. Because of this, it was also known as the Karakoram route. The Karakoram mountain range spans the borders of Pakistan, India, and China, and also extends into Afghanistan and Tajikistan in the northwest.

West of the Karakoram mountains, the southern route had many spurs heading south to the sea, since many travellers wished to continue by ship instead of going overland.

For those who did not head south to the ocean, the southern route continued over the

Hindu Kush mountains and into Afghanistan, joining the northern routes before reaching Merv in Turkmenistan.

From Merv, the southern route went westward in almost a straight line, through northern Iran, Mesopotamia and the northern outskirts of the Syrian Desert, to reach the Levant where ships were waiting to take the precious cargo across the Mediterranean to southern Europe. Continued travel over land was also possible from the Levant, either north through Anatolia or south to North Africa.

There was also a branch of the Silk Road that went from Herat in Afghanistan to the ancient port town of Charax Spasinu by the Persian Gulf, passing through Susa on the way. From Charax Spasinu, the journey continued by ship to various Mediterranean ports, such as Petra.

The Southwestern Route

The southwestern route went from China to India, through the Ganges Delta. This delta region was an important trading hub, and archaeological excavations have found an astonishing array of goods from various parts of the world here, such as ancient Roman beads and gemstones from Thailand and Java.

Trading hub: The regions role as a trading hub also meant that the area served as a currency exchange. Most western currencies never made it further east than this and most eastern and Chinese coins never made it further west than this. The traders in the Ganges Delta primarily used eastern currencies when they traded with eastern merchants and western currencies when they traded with western merchants. Traders would exchange currency with each-other to have the appropriate currency when trading with merchants from different areas. This was not strictly speaking necessary since the coins were made out of precious metals and their worth was determined by their gold or silver value. Many traders would none the less prefer to trade using currencies that was widely circulated in their part of the world. IE Western traders preferred the silver drachm of the Sasanian empire (Neo-Persian) or the gold solidus of the Byzantine empire (Eastern Rome) and eastern traders preferred Chinese currency.

Currency brokers: The traders in the Ganges Delta did in other words fill a function similar to what currency exchange brokers do today. Currency brokers help facilitate the trade between different countries and cultures by allowing people to buy and sell currencies. Today these brokers also facilitate currency speculation and trading. The buying and selling of currencies to make a profit from changes in the exchange rate. This was not possible at the time of the silk road since, as earlier mention, the value of the currencies was fixed to the value of the metals they were made of.

The Ledo Route

There is evidence for a trading route going from Sichuan in modern-day China through Yunnan, Burma, and Bangladesh. In some sources, the route is called Ledo.

Even though the ancient Greco-Roman geographer Claudius Ptolemy (circa 100 AD—170 AD) never travelled this far east, he must have been able to obtain information about the region through other travellers, because he produced a map where the Ganges Delta is depicted with a remarkable degree of accuracy. The map shows that whoever informed Ptolemy knew about things such as the course of the Brahmaputra River.

Maritime routes

The maritime parts of the Silk Road involved waters such as:
- The Yellow Sea
- The East China Sea
- The South China Sea
- The Strait of Malacca
- The Indian Ocean
- The Gulf of Bengal
- The Arabian Sea
- The Persian Gulf
- The Red Sea
- The Mediterranean

Silk Fabric

Silk fabric was first developed in ancient China. The earliest example of silk fabric is from 3630 BC, and it was used as wrapping for the body of a child from a Yangshao culture site in Qingtaicun at Xingyang, Henan.

Legend gives credit for developing silk to a Chinese empress, Leizu (Hsi-Ling-Shih, Lei-Tzu). Silks were originally reserved for the Emperors of China for their own use and gifts to others, but spread gradually through Chinese culture and trade both geographically and socially, and then to many regions of Asia. Because of its texture and lustre, silk rapidly became a popular luxury fabric in the many areas accessible to Chinese merchants. Silk was in great demand, and became a staple of pre-industrial international trade. In July 2007, archaeologists discovered intricately woven and dyed silk textiles in a tomb in Jiangxi province, dated to the Eastern Zhou Dynasty roughly 2500 years ago. Although historians have suspected a long history of a formative textile industry in ancient China, this find of silk textiles employing "complicated techniques" of weaving and dyeing provides direct evidence for silks dating before the Mawangdui-discovery and other silks dating to the Han Dynasty.

Silk is described in a chapter on *Mulberry Planting* by Si Shengzhi of the Western Han (206 BC—9 AD). There is a surviving calendar for silk production in an Eastern Han document. The two other known works on silk from the Han period are lost. The first evidence of the long distance silk trade is the finding of silk in the hair of an Egyptian mummy of the 21st dynasty, c.1070 BC. The silk trade reached as far as the Indian subcontinent, the Middle East, Europe, and North Africa. This trade is so extensive that the major set of trade routes between Europe and Asia come to be known as the Silk Road.

The Emperors of China strove to keep knowledge of sericulture secret to maintain the

Chinese monopoly. Nonetheless sericulture reached Korea with technological aid from China around 200 BC the ancient Kingdom of Khotan by 50 AD, and India by 140 AD. In the ancient era, silk from China was the most lucrative and sought-after luxury item traded across the Eurasian continent, and many civilizations, such as the ancient Persians, benefited economically from trade.

Properties

Silk fibers from the *Bombyx mori* silkworm have a triangular cross section with rounded corners, 5~10μm wide. The fibroin-heavy chain is composed mostly of beta-sheets, due to a 59-mer amino acid repeat sequence with some variations. The flat surfaces of the fibrils reflect light at many angles, giving silk a natural sheen. The cross-section from other silkworms can vary in shape and diameter: crescent-like for *Anaphe* and elongated wedge for *tussah*. Silkworm fibers are naturally extruded from two silkworm glands as a pair of primary filaments (brin), which are stuck together, with sericin proteins that actlike glue, to form a bave. Bave diameters for tussah silk can reach 65μm. Seecited reference for cross-sectional SEM photographs.

Silk has a smooth, soft texture that is not slippery, unlike many synthetic fibers. Silk is one of the strongest natural fibers, but it loses up to 20% of its strength when wet. It has a good moisture regain of 11%. Its elasticity is moderate to poor: if elongated even a small amount, it remains stretched. It can be weakened if exposed to too much sunlight. It may also be attacked by insects, especially if left dirty.

Silk is a poor conductor of electricity. One example of the durable nature of silk over other fabrics is demonstrated by the recovery in 1840 of silk garments: "The most durablearticle found has been silk; for besides pieces of cloaks and lace, a pair of blacksatin breeches, and a large satin waistcoat with flaps, were got up, of which the silk was perfect, but the lining entirely gone... from the thread giving way... No articles of dress of woollen cloth have yet been found."

Unwashed silk chiffon may shrink up to 8% due to a relaxation of the fiber macro structure, so silk should either be washed prior to garment construction, or dry cleaned. Dry cleaning may still shrink the chiffon up to 4%. Occasionally, this shrinkage can be reversed by a gentle steaming with a press cloth. There is almost no gradual shrinkage nor shrinkage due to molecular-level deformation. Natural and synthetic silk is known to manifest piezoelectric properties in proteins, probably due to its molecular structure.

Silkworm silk was used as the standard for the denier, a measurement of linear density in fibers. Silkworm silk therefore has alinear density of approximately 1 den, or 1.1 d tex.

Comparison of silk fibers	Linear density (d tex)	Diameter (μm)	Coeff. variation
Moth: *Bombyx mori*	1.17	12.9	24.8%
Spider: *Argiope aurentia*	0.14	3.57	14.8%

Chemical properties

Silk emitted by the silkworm consists of two main proteins, sericin and fibroin,

fibroin being the structural center of the silk, andserecin being the sticky material surrounding it. Fibroin is made up of the amino acids Gly-Ser-Gly-Ala-Gly-Ala and forms beta pleated sheets. Hydrogen bonds form between chains, and side chains form above and below the plane of the hydrogenbond network.

The high proportion (50%) of glycine allows tight packing. This is because glycine's R group is only a hydrogen and so is not assterically constrained. The addition of alanine and serine makes the fibres strong and resistant to breaking. This tensile streng this due to the many interceded hydrogen bonds, and when stretched the force is applied to these numerous bonds and they do not break.

Silk is resistant to most mineral acids, except for sulfuric acid, which dissolves it. It is yellowed by perspiration. Chlorine bleach will also destroy silk fabrics.

Uses

Silk's absorbency makes it comfortable to wear in warm weather and while active. Its low conductivity keeps warm air close to the skin during cold weather. It is often used for clothing such as shirts, ties, blouses, formal dresses, high fashion clothes, lining, lingerie, pajamas, robes, dress suits, sun dresses and Eastern folk costumes. For practical use, silk is excellent as clothing that protects from many biting insects that would ordinarily pierce clothing, such as mosquitoes and horseflies. Silk's attractive lustre and drape makes it suitable for many furnishing applications. It is used for upholstery, wall coverings, window treatments (if blended with another fiber), rugs, bedding and wall hangings. While on the decline now, due to artificial fibers, silk has had many industrial and commercial uses, such as in parachutes, bicycle tires, comforter filling and artillery gunpowder bags.

Fabrics that are often made from silk include charmeuse, habutai, chiffon, taffeta, crepe de chine, dupioni, noil, tussah, and shantung, among others.

A special manufacturing process removes the outer sericin coating of the silk, which makes it suitable as non-absorbable surgical sutures. This process has also recently led to the introduction of specialist silk underclothing that can significantly reduce eczema. New uses and manufacturing techniques have been found for silk for making everything from disposable cups to drug delivery systems and holograms.

Applications as a biomaterial

Silk has been considered as a luxurious textile since 3630 BC. However, it started to serve also as a biomedical material for suture in surgeries decades ago. In the past 30 years, it has been widely studied and used as a biomaterial, which refers tomaterials used for medical applications in organisms, due to its excellent properties, including remarkable mechanical properties, comparative biocompatibility, tunable degradation rates *in vitro* and *in vivo*, the ease to load cellular growth factors(for example, BMP-2), and the ability to be processed into several other formats such as films, gels, particles, and scaffolds. Silks from

Bombyx mori, a kind of cultivated silkworm, are the most widely investigated silks.

Silks derived from *Bombyx mori* are generally made of two parts: the silk fibroin fiber which contains a light chain of 25kDa anda heavy chain of 350kDa (or 390kDa) linked by a single disulfide bond and a glue-like protein, sericin, comprising 25 to 30 percentage by weight. Silk fibroin contains hydrophobic Beta sheet blocks, interrupted by small hydrophilic groups. And the beta-sheets contribute much to the high mechanical strength of silk fibers, which achieves 740MPa, tens of times that of poly(lactic acid) and hundreds of times that of collagen. This impressive mechanical strength has made silk fibroin very competitive for applications in biomaterials. Indeed, silk fibers have found their way into tendon tissue engineering, where mechanical properties matter greatly. In addition, mechanical properties of silks from various kinds of silkworms vary widely, which provides more choices for their use in tissue engineering.

Most products fabricated from regenerated silk are weak and brittle, due to the absence of appropriate secondary and hierarchical structure.

Biocompatibility, i.e., the ability to what level the silk will cause an immune response, is definitely a critical issue for biomaterials. The biocompatibility of silk arose during its increasing clinical use. Indeed, wax or silicone is usually used as a coating to avoid fraying and potential immune responses when silk fibers serve as suture materials. Although the lack of detailed characterization of silk fibers, such as the extent of the removal of sericin, the surface chemical properties of coating material, and the process used, make it difficult to determine the real immune response of silk fibers in literature, it is generally believed that sericin is the major cause of immune response. Thus, the removal of sericin is an essential step to assure biocompatibility in biomaterial applications of silk. However, further research fails to prove clearly the contribution of sericin to inflammatory responses based on isolated sericin and sericin based biomaterials. In addition, silk fibroin exhibits an inflammatory response similar to that of tissue culture plastic *in vitro* when assessed with human mesenchymal stem cells (hMSCs) or lower than collagen and PLA when implant rat MSCs with silk fibroin films *in vivo*. Thus, appropriate degumming andsterilization will assure the biocompatibility of silk fibroin, which is further validated by *in vivo* experiments on rats and pigs. There are still concerns about the long-term safety of silk-based biomaterials in the human body in contrast to these promisingresults. Even though silk sutures serve well, they exist and interact within a limited period depending on the recovery of wounds(several weeks), much shorter than that in tissue engineering. Another concern arises from biodegradation because the biocompatibility of silk fibroin does not necessarily assure the biocompatibility of the decomposed products. In fact, different levels of immune responses and diseases have been triggered by the degraded products of silk fibroin.

Myths and Legends of Silk

In China, a legend indicates the discovery of the silkworm's silk was by an ancient empress named Leizu, the wife of the Yellow Emperor, also known as Xi Lingshi. She was drinking tea under a tree when a silk cocoon fell into her tea. As she picked it out and started to wrap the silk thread around her finger, she slowly felt a warm sensation. When the silk ran out, she saw a small larva. In an instant, she realized this caterpillar larva was the source of the silk. She taught this to the people and it became widespread. Many more legends about the silkworm are told.

The Chinese guarded their knowledge of silk, but, according to one story, a Chinese princess given in marriage to a Khotan prince brought to the oasis the secret of silk manufacture, "hiding silkworms in her hair as part of her dowry", probably in the first half of the 1st century AD. About 550 AD, Christian monks were said to have smuggled silkworms, in a hollow stick, out of China and sold the secret to the Byzantine Empire.

Leizu, also known as Xi Lingshi (西陵氏, Wade–Giles Hsi Ling-shih), was a legendary Chinese empress and wife of the Yellow Emperor. According to tradition, she discovered sericulture, and invented the silk loom, in the 27th century BC. Leizu discovered silkworms while having an afternoon tea, and a cocoon fell in her tea. It slowly unraveled and she was enchanted by it.

According to one the writings of Confucius and Chinese tradition recount that, in the 27th century BC, a silkworm cocoon fell into her tea, and the heat unwrapped the silk until it stretched across her entire garden. When the silk ran out, she saw a small cocoon and realized that this cocoon was the source of the silk. Another version says that she found silkworms eating the mulberry leaves and spinning cocoons. She collected some cocoons, then sat down to have some tea. While she was sipping a cup, she dropped a cocoon into the steaming water. A fine thread started to separate itself from the milk worm cocoon. Leizu found that she could unwind this soft and lovely thread around her finger.

She persuaded her husband to give her a grove of mulberry trees, where she could domesticate the worms that made these cocoons. She was attributed with inventing the silk reel, which joined fine filaments into a thread strong enough for weaving. She was also credited with inventing the first silk loom. It is not known how much, if any, of this story is true, but historians do know that China was the first civilization to use silk. Leizu shared her discoveries with others, and the knowledge became widespread in China. She is a popular object of worship in modern China, with the title of "Silkworm Mother" (Can Nainai).

Leizu had a son named Changyi with the Yellow Emperor, and he was the father of Emperor Zhuanxu. Zhuanxu's uncles and his father, the sons of Huangdi, were bypassed and Zhuanxu was selected as heir to Huangdi.

A lacquerware painting from the JingmenTomb (荆门楚墓) of the State of Chu (704 BC —223 BC), depicting men wearing precursors to Hanfu(i.e. traditional silk dress) and riding in a two-horsed chariot.

Silk eventually left China via the heir of a princess who was promised to a prince of Khotan. This probably occurred in the early 1st century AD. The princess, refusing to go without the fabric that she loved, would finally break the imperial ban on silk-worm exportation.

Though silk was exported to foreign countries in great amounts, sericulture remained a secret that the Chinese carefully guarded. Consequently, other people invented wildly varying accounts of the source of the incredible fabric.

In classical antiquity, most Romans, great admirers of the cloth, were convinced that the Chinese took the fabric from tree leaves. This belief was affirmed by Seneca the Elder in his *Phaedra* and by Virgil in his *Georgics*. Notably, Pliny the Elder knew better. Speaking of the bombyx or silk moth, he wrote in his *Natural History* "they weave webs, like spiders, that become a luxurious clothing material for women, called silk".

Woven silk textile from Tomb No. 1 at Mawangdui Han tombs site, Changsha, Hunan province, China, 2nd century BC, Western Han Dynasty.

In China, silk-worm farming was originally restricted to women, and many women were employed in the silk-making industry. Even though some saw the development of a luxury product as useless, silk provoked such a craze among high society that the rules in the Li Ji were used to limit its use to the members of the imperial family. For approximately a millennium, the right to wear silk was reserved for the emperor and the highest dignitaries. Silk was, at the time, a sign of great wealth, because of its shimmering appearance. This appearance was due to silk's prism-like shape/structure, which refracted light from every angle. After some time, silk gradually extended to other classes of Chinese society. Silk began to be used for decorative means and also in less luxurious ways: musical instruments, fishing, and bow making. Peasants did not have the right to wear silk until the Qing dynasty.

Paper was one of the greatest discoveries of ancient China. Beginning in the 3rd century BC paper was made in all sizes with various materials. Silk was no exception, and silk workers had been making paper since the 2nd century BC. Silk, bamboo, linen, wheat and rice straw were all used differently, and paper made with silk became the first type of luxury paper. Researchers have found an early example of writing done on silk paper in the tomb of a Marchioness who died around 168, in Mawangdui, Changsha, Hunan. The material was certainly more expensive, but also more practical than bamboo slips. Treatises on many subjects, including meteorology, medicine, astrology, divinity, and even maps written on silk have been discovered.

Words & Expressions

limnic /ˈlɪmnɪk/ *adj.* 湖泊的，湖沼的，湖栖的
fibroin /ˈfaɪbroʊɪn/ *n.* 蚕丝蛋白
myrrh /mɜːr/ *n.* 没药（热带树脂，可作香料、药材）；[植] 没药树
frankincense /ˈfræŋkɪnsens/ *n.* 乳香
chrysanthemums /krɪˈsænθəməmz/ *n.* 菊花（chrysanthemum 的复数）
lacquer ware 漆器

Notes

The term is used for both overland routes and those that are marine or limnic. The Silk Road is named after the lucrative international trade in Chinese silk textiles that started during the Han dynasty (207 BC—220 AD).

这个词用于陆路航线和海湖航线。丝绸之路是以汉代（公元前 207—公元 220）开始的利润丰厚的中国丝绸纺织品国际贸易命名的。

Reading Comprehension

Ⅰ. Each piece of the following information is given in one of the paragraphs in the passage. Identify the paragraph from which the information is derived and put the corresponding number in the space provided.

(　　) 1. Porcelain from China were traded along the Silk Road.
(　　) 2. The Silk Road includes overland, marine or limnic routes.
(　　) 3. The Silk Road consisted of more than three routes.
(　　) 4. Chang'an was the eastern most point of the northern route.
(　　) 5. Silk and other goods were traded along the Silk Road for the expansion and spread of religion, philosophy, technology, and artistic ideals.
(　　) 6. It seems to be unusual for any merchant to trade between China and Europe or Northern Africa.

Ⅱ. Decide whether the statements are true (T) or false (F) according to the passage.

(　　) 1. The Chinese Emperor around the first century prevented nomadic tribes from attacking along the northern route.
(　　) 2. The southwestern route went from China to Indonesia, through the Ganges Delta.
(　　) 3. Most western currencies never made it further east than this and most eastern and Chinese coins never made it further west than this.
(　　) 4. Currency brokers help facilitate the trade between different nations by forbidding people to trade currencies.
(　　) 5. It is a modern invention to adopt one single name the Silk Road for the intricate web of trade routes.

Development

Ⅲ. Discuss the following questions.

1. What are the characteristics of marine route of the Silk Road?
2. Do you have more insights into trade routes in ancient times beside the Silk Road?

第八章 稻

Chapter 8 Rice

Text A 稻 About Rice

Rice is the seed of the grass species *Oryza sativa* (Asian rice) or *Oryza glaberrima* (African rice). As a cereal grain, it is the most widely consumed staple food for a large part of the world's human population, especially in Asia. It is the agricultural commodity with the third-highest worldwide production (rice, 741.5 million tonnes in 2014), after sugarcane (1.9 billion tonnes) and maize (1.0 billion tonnes).

Since sizable portions of sugarcane and maize crops are used for purposes other than human consumption, rice is the most important grain with regard to human nutrition and caloric intake, providing more than one-fifth of the calories consumed worldwide by humans. There are many varieties of rice and culinary preferences tend to vary regionally.

Rice, a monocot, is normally grown as an annual plant, although in tropical areas it can survive as a perennial and can produce a ratoon crop for up to 30 years. Rice cultivation is well-suited to countries and regions with low labor costs and high rainfall, as it is labor-intensive to cultivate and requires ample water. However, rice can be grown practically anywhere, even on a steep hill or mountain area with the use of water-controlling terrace systems. Although its parent species are native to Asia and certain parts of Africa, centuries of trade and exportation have made it commonplace in many cultures worldwide.

The traditional method for cultivating rice is flooding the fields while, or after, setting the young seedlings. This simple method requires sound planning and servicing of the water damming and channeling, but reduces the growth of less robust weed and pest plants that have no submerged growth state, and deters vermin. While flooding is not mandatory for the cultivation of rice, all other methods of irrigation require higher effort in weed and pest control during growth periods and a different approach for fertilizing the soil.

Rice requires high temperature above 20℃ (68 °F) but not more than 35~40℃ (95~104°F). Optimum temperature is around 30℃ (T_{max}) and 20℃ (T_{min}). The amount of solar radiation received during the 45 days leading up to harvest determines final crop output. High water vapor content (in humid tropics) subjects unusual stress which favors the spread of fungal and bacterial diseases. Light wind transports CO_2 to the leaf canopy but strong wind causes severe damage and may lead to sterility (due to pollen dehydration, spikelet sterility, and abortive endosperms).

Amid the wugu, rice is the most widely consumed staple food for Chinese people. So far, there has been no agreement on the exact time and location of rice domestication. A 2012 study published in the journal *Nature* indicated that the domestication of rice occurred in the Pearl River Valley region of China. From East Asia, rice was spread to South and Southeast Asia. Before this research, the commonly accepted view was that rice was first domesticated in the region of the Yangtze River Valley in China. Archaeological discoveries at the Diaotonghuan Site in Jiangxi Province clearly show the transition from the collection of wild rice to the cultivation of domesticated rice, which indicate that wild rice collection was part of the local means of subsistence from 12000 BC—11000 BC with rice gradually domesticated between 10000 BC—8000 BC In spite of the disputes, rice is considered to have been planted around 10000 years before in China.

During the Neolithic Age, rice grew mainly in south China. The following 2000 years from the Xia Dynasty to the Han Dynasty witnessed rice cultivated in both south and north China. According to *The Book of Rites* a special official was assigned by the central government to take charge of developing rice cultivation in seven of the nine states, of which fire states were in North China. Written records showed that the biennial rice was already cultivated during the Han Dynasty in Guangdong Province and Guangxi Zhuang Autonomous Region.

During the Tang Dynasty, rice spread to western, northwestern and northeastern China. According to *Kuo Dizhi*, a book on geography, in the south of Kun Lun Mountains which located in Western China, a piece of fertile land was stretched with rice as the staple crop. At the time, rice was also widely cultivated in Yunnan Province in southwestern China, from which rice noodles with special flavors, namely guoqiao mixian (literally means "noodles crossing the bridge"), spread and became popular across the country.

Rice cultivation was actively promoted in the Song Dynasty. Large areas in provinces of Hebei and Henan were turned into paddy fields. Water engineering was encouraged to control floods and to irrigate fields, thus considerably improving productivity.

In the mid-eighteenth century, rice was even spread to what are now Xingjiang Uygur Autonomous Region and Tibet Autonomous Region. The Ming and Qing Dynasties from 1368~1911 saw rice cultivated almost across the whole country. Biennial rice was widely grown in South China. In some warm regions rice was even harvested three times a year.

With the widespread adoption and popularity of rice, it began to change daily life and traditions. On the eve of Chinese lunar new year, niangao, made of glutinous rice is a must for family gathering. It is considered good luck to eat niangao since it sounds similar to (年高) which means "better life year by year" and "longevity".

Besides niangao, another festival food made of rice is zongzi. To celebrate the Dragon Boat Festival, people wrapped glutinous rice with reed leaves. Zongzi is said to be prepared in honor of Qu Yuan, a famous poet and loyal official to the ruler of kingdom Chu during the Warring States Period.

Domestication of Rice

Chinese legends attribute the domestication of rice to Shennong, the legendary emperor of China and inventor of Chinese agriculture. Genetic evidence has shown that rice originates from a single domestication 8200~13500 years ago in the Pearl River Valley region of Ancient China. Previously, archaeological evidence had suggested that rice was domesticated in the Yangtze River Valley region in China. From East Asia, rice was spread to Southeast and South Asia. Rice was introduced to Europe through Western Asia, and to the Americas through European colonization.

There have been many debates on the origins of the domesticated rice. Genetic evidence published in the *Proceedings of the National Academy of Sciences* of the United States of America (*PNAS*) shows that all forms of Asian rice, both indica and japonica, spring from a single domestication that occurred 8200~13500 years ago in China of the wild rice *Oryza rufipogon*. A 2012 study published in *Nature*, through a map of rice genome variation, indicated that the domestication of rice occurred in the Pearl River valley region of China based on the genetic evidence. From East Asia, rice was spread to South and Southeast Asia. Before this research, the commonly accepted view, based on archaeological evidence, was that rice was first domesticated in the region of the Yangtze River Valley in China.

Morphological studies of rice phytoliths from the Diaotonghuan archaeological site clearly show the transition from the collection of wild rice to the cultivation of domesticated rice. The large number of wild rice phytoliths at the Diaotonghuan level dating from 12000 BC—11000 BC indicates that wild rice collection was part of the local means of subsistence. Changes in the morphology of Diaotonghuan phytoliths dating from 10000 BC—8000 BC show that rice had by this time been domesticated. Soon afterwards the two major varieties of indica and japonica rice were being grown in Central China. In the late 3rd millennium BC, there was a rapid expansion of rice cultivation into mainland Southeast Asia and westwards across India and Nepal.

In 2003, archaeologists claimed to have discovered the world's oldest domesticated rice. Their 15000-year-old age challenges the accepted view that rice cultivation originated in China about 12000 years ago. These findings were received by academia with strong skepticism, and the results and their publicizing has been cited as being driven by a combination of nationalist and regional interests. In 2011, a combined effort by the Stanford University, New York University, Washington University in St. Louis, and Purdue University has provided the strongest evidence yet that there is only one single origin of domesticated rice, in the Yangtze Valley of China.

Rice spread to the Middle East where, according to Zohary and Hopf, *O. sativa* was recovered from a grave at Susa in Iran (dated to the 1st century AD).

The current scientific consensus, based on archaeological and linguistic evidence, is that rice was first domesticated in the Yangtze River basin in China. Because the functional allele for nonshattering, the critical indicator of domestication in grains, as well as five other single-nucleotide polymorphisms, is identical in both indica and japonica, Vaughan et al. (2008) determined a single domestication event for *O. sativa*. This was supported by a genetic study in 2011 that showed that all forms of Asian rice, both indica and japonica, sprang from a single domestication event that occurred 13500 to 8200 years ago in China from the wild rice *Oryza rufipogon*. A more recent population genomic study indicates that japonica was domesticated first, and that indica rice arose when japonica arrived in India about 4500 years ago and hybridized with an undomesticated proto-indica or wild *O. nivara*.

There are two most likely centers of domestication for rice as well as the development of the wetland agriculture technology. The first, and most likely, is in the lower Yangtze River, believed to be the homelands of the pre-Austronesians and possibly also the Kra-Dai, and associated with the Kauhuqiao, Hemudu, Majiabang, Songze, Liangzhu, and Maquiao cultures. It is characterized by pre-Austronesian features, including stilt houses, jade carving, and boat technologies. Their diet were also supplemented by acorns, water chestnuts, foxnuts, and pig domestication.

The second is in the middle Yangtze River, believed to be the homelands of the early Hmong-Mien-speakers and associated with the Pengtoushan, Nanmuyuan, Liulinxi, Daxi, Qujialing, and Shijiahe cultures. Both of these regions were heavily populated and had regular trade contacts with each other, as well as with early Austroasiatic speakers to the west, and early Kra-Dai speakers to the south, facilitating the spread of rice cultivation throughout southern China.

Rice was gradually introduced north into early Sino-Tibetan Yangshao and Dawenkou culture millet farmers, either via contact with the Daxi culture or the Majiabang-Hemudu culture. By around 4000 to 3800 BC, they were a regular secondary crop among southernmost Sino-Tibetan cultures. It did not replace millet, largely because of different environment conditions in northern China, but it was cultivated alongside millet in the southern boundaries of the millet-farming regions. Conversely, millet was also introduced into rice-farming regions.

By the late Neolithic (3500—2500 BC), population in the rice cultivating centers had increased rapidly, centered around the Qujialing-Shijiahe culture and the Liangzhu culture. There was also evidence of intensive rice cultivation in paddy fields as well as increasingly sophisticated material cultures in these two regions. The number of settlements among the Yangtze cultures and their sizes increased, leading some archaeologists to characterize them as true states, with clearly advanced socio-political structures. However, it is unknown if they had centralized control.

Liangzhu and Shijiahe declined abruptly in the terminal Neolithic (2500 to 2000 BC). With Shijiahe shrinking in size, and Liangzhu disappearing altogether. This is largely believed to be the result of the southward expansion of the early Sino-Tibetan Longshan culture. Fortifications like walls (as well as extensive moats in Liangzhu cities) are common features in settlements during this period, indicating widespread conflict. This period also coincides with the southward movement of rice-farming cultures to the Lingnan and Fujian regions, as well as the southward migrations of the Austronesian, Kra-Dai, and Austroasiatic-speaking peoples to Mainland Southeast Asia and Island Southeast Asia.

Production of Rice

Rice production in China is an important part of the national economy. China is the world's largest producer of rice, and the crop makes up a little less than half of the country's total grain output. China accounts for 30% of all world rice production. In a given year total rice output came from four different crops. The early rice crop grows primarily in provinces along the Yangtze River and in provinces in the south, it is planted in February to April and harvested in June and July and contributes about 34% to total rice output. Intermediate and single-crop late rice grows in the southwest and along the Yangtze, it is planted in March to June and harvested in October and November and also contributed about 34% to total rice output in the 1980s. Double-crop late rice, planted after the early crop is reaped, is harvested in October to November and adds about 25% to total rice production. Rice grown in the north is planted from April to June and harvested from September to October, it contributes about 7% to total production.

All rice cultivation is highly labour intensive. Rice is generally grown as a wetland crop in fields flooded to supply water during the growing season. Transplanting seedlings requires many hours of labor, as does harvesting. Mechanization of rice cultivation is only minimally advanced. Rice cultivation also demands more of other inputs, such as fertilizer, than most other crops.

Rice is highly prized by consumers as a food grain, especially in south China, and per capita consumption has risen through the years. Also, as incomes have risen, consumers have preferred to eat more rice and less potatoes, corn, sorghum, and millet. Large production increased in the early 1980s and poor local transportation systems combined to induce farmers to feed large quantities of lower quality rice to livestock.

Production and commerce

In 2014, world production of paddy rice was 741.5 million tonnes, led by China and India with a combined 49% of this total. Other major producers were Indonesia,

Bangladesh and Vietnam. The average world farm yield for rice in 2014 was 4.6 tonnes per hectare. Rice farms in France were the most productive in 2014, with a nationwide average of 50.1 tonnes per hectare.

Rice is a major food staple and a mainstay for the rural population and their food security. It is mainly cultivated by small farmers in holdings of less than 1 hectare. Rice is also a wage commodity for workers in the cash crop or non-agricultural sectors. Rice is vital for the nutrition of much of the population in Asia, as well as in Latin America and the Caribbean and in Africa; it is central to the food security of over half the world population. Developing countries account for 95% of the total production, with China and India alone responsible for nearly half of the world output.

Many rice grain producing countries have significant losses post-harvest at the farm and because of poor roads, inadequate storage technologies, inefficient supply chains and farmer's inability to bring the produce into retail markets dominated by small shopkeepers. A World Bank—FAO study claims 8% to 26% of rice is lost in developing nations, on average, every year, because of post-harvest problems and poor infrastructure. Some sources claim the post-harvest losses to exceed 40%. Not only do these losses reduce food security in the world, the study claims that farmers in developing countries such as China, India and others lose approximately US$89 billion of income in preventable post-harvest farm losses, poor transport, the lack of proper storage and retail. One study claims that if these post-harvest grain losses could be eliminated with better infrastructure and retail network, in India alone enough food would be saved every year to feed 70 to 100 million people over a year.

Processing

The seeds of the rice plant are first milled using a rice huller to remove the chaff (the outer husks of the grain). At this point in the process, the product is called brown rice. The milling may be continued, removing the bran, i.e., the rest of the husk and the germ, thereby creating white rice. White rice, which keeps longer, lacks some important nutrients; moreover, in a limited diet which does not supplement the rice, brown rice helps to prevent the disease beriberi.

Either by hand or in a rice polisher, white rice may be buffed with glucose or talc powder (often called polished rice, though this term may also refer to white rice in general), parboiled, or processed into flour. White rice may also be enriched by adding nutrients, especially those lost during the milling process. While the cheapest method of enriching involves adding a powdered blend of nutrients that will easily wash off (in the United States, rice which has been so treated requires a label warning against rinsing), more sophisticated methods apply nutrients directly to the grain, coating the grain with a water-insoluble substance which is resistant to washing.

In some countries, a popular form, parboiled rice (also known as converted rice) is subjected to a steaming or parboiling process while still a brown rice grain. The parboil process causes a gelatinisation of the starch in the grains. The grains become less brittle, and the color of the milled grain changes from white to yellow. The rice is then dried, and can then be milled as usual or used as brown rice. Milled parboiled rice is nutritionally superior to standard milled rice, because the process causes nutrients from the outer husk (especially thiamine) to move into the endosperm, so that less is subsequently lost when the husk is polished off during milling. Parboiled rice has an additional benefit in that it does not stick to the pan during cooking, as happens when cooking regular white rice. This type of rice is eaten in parts of India and countries of West Africa are also accustomed to consuming parboiled rice.

Rice is a good source of protein and a staple food in many parts of the world, but it is not a complete protein: it does not contain all of the essential amino acids in sufficient amounts for good health, and should be combined with other sources of protein, such as nuts, seeds, beans, fish, or meat.

Rice, like other cereal grains, can be puffed (or popped). This process takes advantage of the grains' water content and typically involves heating grains in a special chamber. Further puffing is sometimes accomplished by processing puffed pellets in a low-pressure chamber. The ideal gas law means either lowering the local pressure or raising the water temperature results in an increase in volume prior to water evaporation, resulting in a puffy texture. Bulk raw rice density is about $0.9g/cm^3$. It decreases to less than one-tenth that when puffed.

Harvesting, drying and milling

Unmilled rice, known as "paddy" is usually harvested when the grains have a moisture content of around 25%. In most Asian countries, where rice is almost entirely the product of smallholder agriculture, harvesting is carried out manually, although there is a growing interest in mechanical harvesting. Harvesting can be carried out by the farmers themselves, but is also frequently done by seasonal labor groups. Harvesting is followed by threshing, either immediately or within a day or two. Again, much threshing is still carried out by hand but there is an increasing use of mechanical threshers. Subsequently, paddy needs to be dried to bring down the moisture content to no more than 20% for milling.

A familiar sight in several Asian countries is paddy laid out to dry along roads. However, in most countries the bulk of drying of marketed paddy takes place in mills, with village-level drying being used for paddy to be consumed by farm families. Mills either sun dry or use mechanical driers or both. Drying has to be carried out quickly to avoid the formation of molds. Mills range from simple hullers, with a throughput of a couple of tonnes a day, that simply remove the outer husk, to enormous operations that can process 4000 tonnes a day and produce highly polished rice. A good mill can achieve a paddy-to-rice conversion rate of up to 72% but smaller, inefficient mills often struggle to achieve 60%. These smaller mills often do not buy paddy and sell rice but only service farmers who want to mill their paddy for their own consumption.

Trade

World trade figures are very different from those for production, as less than 8% of rice produced is traded internationally. In economic terms, the global rice trade was a small fraction of 1% of world mercantile trade. Many countries consider rice as a strategic food staple, and various governments subject its trade to a wide range of controls and interventions.

Developing countries are the main players in the world rice trade, accounting for 83% of exports and 85% of imports. While there are numerous importers of rice, the exporters of rice are limited. Just five countries—Thailand, Vietnam, China, the United States and India—in decreasing order of exported quantities, accounted for about three-quarters of world rice exports in 2002. However, this ranking has been rapidly changing in recent years. In 2010, the three largest exporters of rice, in decreasing order of quantity exported were Thailand, Vietnam and India. By 2012, India became the largest exporter of rice with a 100% increase in its exports on year-to-year basis, and Thailand slipped to third position. Together, Thailand, Vietnam and India accounted for nearly 70% of the world rice exports.

The primary variety exported by Thailand and Vietnam were jasmine rice, while exports from India included aromatic Basmativariety. China, an exporter of rice in early 2000s, was a net importer of rice in 2010 and would become the largest net importer, surpassing Nigeria, in 2013. According to a USDA report, the world's largest exporters of rice in 2012 were India (9.75 million tonnes), Vietnam (7 million tonnes), Thailand (6.5 million tonnes), Pakistan (3.75 million tonnes) and the United States(3.5 million tonnes).

The average world yield for rice was 4.3 tonnes per hectare, in 2010. Yuan Longping of China National Hybrid Rice Research and Development Center, China, set a world record for rice yield in 2010 at 19 tonnes per hectare on a demonstration plot. In 2011, this record was surpassed by an Indian farmer, Sumant Kumar, with 22.4 tonnes per hectare in Bihar. Both these farmers claim to have employed newly developed rice breeds and System of Rice Intensification (SRI), a recent innovation in rice farming. SRI is claimed to have set new national records in rice yields, within the last 10 years, in many countries. The claimed Chinese and Indian yields have yet to be demonstrated on seven-hectare lots and to be reproducible over two consecutive years on the same farm.

Environmental impacts

Rice cultivation on wetland rice fields is thought to be responsible for 11% of the anthropogenic methane emissions. Rice requires slightly more water to produce than other grains. Rice production uses almost a third of Earth's fresh water.

Long-term flooding of rice fields cuts the soil off from atmospheric oxygen and causes anaerobic fermentation of organic matter in the soil. Methane production from rice cultivation contributes about 1.5% of anthropogenic greenhouse gases. Methane is twenty times more potent a greenhouse gas than carbon dioxide.

A 2010 study found that, as a result of rising temperatures and decreasing solar radiation during the later years of the 20th century, the rice yield growth rate has decreased in many parts of Asia, compared to what would have been observed had the temperature and solar radiation trends not occurred. The yield growth rate had fallen 10%~20% at some locations. The study was based on records from 227 farms in Thailand, Vietnam, Nepal, India, China, Bangladesh, and Pakistan. The mechanism of this falling yield was not clear, but might involve increased respiration during warm nights, which expends energy without being able to photosynthesize.

Words & Expressions

morphological /ˌmɔːfəˈlɒdʒɪkl/ *adj.* 形态学的
phytolith /ˈfaɪtəlɪθ/ *n.* 植物化石
thiamine /ˈθaɪəmɪn/ *n.* [生化] 硫胺素（维生素 B_1，等于 thiamin）
anthropogenic /ˌænθrəpəʊˈdʒenɪk/ *adj.* 人为的，人类，人类起源的
potent /ˈpəʊtənt/ *adj.* 效力强的
indica and japonica rice 籼粳稻

Notes

Morphological studies of rice phytoliths from the Diaotonghuan archaeological site clearly show the transition from the collection of wild rice to the cultivation of domesticated rice.
调兵环考古遗址水稻植物的形态学研究清楚地表明了从野生水稻采集到驯化水稻种植的转变。

Reading Comprehension

Ⅰ. Each piece of the following information is given in one of the paragraphs in the passage. Identify the paragraph from which the information is derived and put the corresponding number in the space provided.

　　(　　) 1. During the Tang Dynasty, rice spread to the west of China.
　　(　　) 2. Rice is the high agricultural product in the world.
　　(　　) 3. As for the approach of cultivating rice, flooding is traditional and simple, however, not mandatory.
　　(　　) 4. Temperature, solar radiation, water and wind are indispensable for rice growth.
　　(　　) 5. Rice was cultivated and harvested three times per year.
　　(　　) 6. As one of most important staple food, Chinese people have been domesticating the rice for over 10000 years.

Ⅱ. Decide whether the statements are true (T) or false (F) according to the passage.

　　(　　) 1. Amid the wugu, rice is a widely consumed staple food for Chinese people.
　　(　　) 2. Rice cultivation is well-suited to countries and regions with high labor costs and

low rainfall.

(　　) 3. As the most important grain with regard to human caloric intake, rice provides more than one-fifth of the nutrition of the people.

(　　) 4. Rice changed the life and traditions of China, since the rice was popularized.

(　　) 5. The approach of flooding the fields while, or after, setting the young seedlings seems good because it requires sound planning and servicing of the water damming and channeling.

Language Focus

III. Complete the sentences with the correct form of the words in the table.

irrigate	species	cereal	pollinate	nutrition
tropical	steep	terrace	native	regionally

1. He also wants to use the water to _____ barren desert land.
2. Fiber is found in _____ foods, beans, fruit and vegetables.
3. Plants get the _____ from the soil in which they grow.
4. He can feel the searing heat of a _____ summer
5. Though the decline started in the 1970s, it became much _____ beginning in 2000.
6. Plants or animals that are _____ to a particular region live or grow there naturally and were not brought there.
7. _____ is used to describe things which relate to a particular area of a country or of the world.
8. _____ are a series of flat areas built like steps on the side of a hill so that crops can be grown there.
9. Many of the indigenous insects are needed to _____ the local plants.
10. Some animal and plant _____ cannot accommodate to the rapidly changing conditions.

IV. Match the sentences in Section A with the English translation in Section B.

Section A
1. 水稻是仅次于甘蔗和小麦的世界第三高产的农产品。
2. 随着水稻的广泛种植，水稻越来越受欢迎，开始改变人们的生活和传统。
3. 水稻在45天中直到收获接受到的太阳照射量决定了其产量。
4. 大米是提供人类营养和热量的最重要谷物。
5. 水稻实际上可以在任何地方种植，甚至在陡峭的山区也可以。

Section B
1. With the widespread adoption and popularity of rice, it began to change daily life and traditions.

2. Rice is the agricultural commodity with the third-highest worldwide production, after sugarcane and maize.

3. Rice is the most important grain with regard to human nutrition and caloric intake.

4. Rice can be grown practically anywhere, even on a steep hill or mountain area.

5. The amount of solar radiation received during the 45 days leading up to harvest determines final crop output.

V. Translate the paragraph into Chinese.

Amid the wugu, rice is the most widely consumed staple food for Chinese people. So far, there has been no agreement on the exact time and location of rice domestication. A 2012 study published in the journal *Nature* indicated that the domestication of rice occurred in the Pearl River Valley region of China. From East Asia, rice was spread to South and Southeast Asia. Before this research, the commonly accepted view was that rice was first domesticated in the region of the Yangtze River Valley in China. Archaeological discoveries at the Diaotonghuan Site in Jiangxi Province clearly show the transition from the collection of wild rice to the cultivation of domesticated rice, which indicate that wild rice collection was part of the local means of subsistence from 12000 BC—11000 BC.

_____

_____

_____

_____

VI. Discuss the following questions.

1. What do you think is the reason that fantastic tales were made up to explain the origin of farming in China?

2. What makes rice popular for the Chinese since the ancient times?

Text B 稻产品 / Main Types of Rice

Glutinous Rice

Glutinous rice (*Oryza sativa* var. *glutinosa*, also called sticky rice, sweet rice or waxy rice) is a type of rice grown mainly in Southeast and East Asia and the eastern parts of South Asia, which has opaque grains, very low amylose content, and is especially sticky when cooked. It is called glutinous in the sense of being glue-like or sticky, and not in the sense of containing gluten. While often called "sticky rice", it differs from non-glutinous strains of japonica rice which also become sticky to some degree when cooked. There are numerous cultivars of glutinous rice, which include japonica, indica, and tropical japonica strains.

In China, glutinous rice has been grown for at least 2000 years. Glutinous rice is also grown in Laos, Thailand, Cambodia, Vietnam, Malaysia, Indonesia, Myanmar, Nepal, Bangladesh, Northeast India, Japan, Korea, and the Philippines. An estimated 85% of Lao rice production is of this type. The rice has been recorded in the region for at least 1100 years.

The improved rice varieties (in terms of yield) adopted throughout Asia during the Green Revolution were non-glutinous, and Lao farmers rejected them in favor of their traditional sticky varieties. Over time, higher-yield strains of glutinous rice have become available from some research programs. By 1999, more than 70% of the area along the Mekong River Valley were of these newer strains.

Glutinous rice is distinguished from other types of rice by having no (or negligible amounts of) amylose, and high amounts of amylopectin (the two components of starch). Amylopectin is responsible for the sticky quality of glutinous rice. The difference has been traced to a single mutation that was selected for by farmers. Like all types of rice, glutinous rice does not contain dietary gluten (i.e. does not containglutenin and gliadin), and should be safe for gluten-free diets.

Glutinous rice can be used either milled or unmilled (that is, with the bran removed or not removed). Milled glutinous rice is white in color and fully opaque (unlike non-glutinous rice varieties, which are somewhat translucent when raw), whereas the bran can give unmilled glutinous rice a purple or black color. Black and purple glutinous rice are distinct strains from white glutinous rice. In developing Asia, there is little regulation, and some governments have issued advisories about toxic dyes being added to colour adulterated rice. Both black and white glutinous rice can be cooked as discrete grains, or ground into flour and cooked as a paste or gel. Sticky rice is used in many recipes throughout Southeast and East Asia.

In the Chinese language, glutinous rice is known as nuomi (糯米). Glutinous rice is also often ground to make glutinous rice flour. This flour is made into niangao and sweet-filled dumplings tangyuan, both of which are commonly eaten at Chinese New Year. It is also used as a thickener and for baking.

Glutinous rice or glutinous rice flour are both used in many Chinese bakery products and in many varieties of dim sum. They produce a flexible, resilient dough, which can take on the flavors of whatever other ingredients are added to it. Cooking usually consists of steaming or boiling, sometimes followed by pan-frying or deep-frying. Sweet glutinous rice is eaten with red bean paste.

Nuomifan (糯米饭), is steamed glutinous rice usually cooked with Chinese sausage, chopped Chinese mushrooms, chopped barbecued pork, and optionally dried shrimp or scallop (the recipe varies depending on the cook's preference).

Zongzi (粽子) is a dumpling consisting of glutinous rice and sweet or savory fillings wrapped in large flat leaves (usually bamboo), which is then boiled or steamed. It is especially eaten during the Dragon Boat Festival, but may be eaten at any time of the year. It is popular as an easily transported snack, or a meal to consume while traveling. It is a common food among Chinese in Hong Kong, Singapore and Malaysia.

Cifangao (糍饭糕) is a popular breakfast food originating in Eastern China consisting of cooked glutinous rice compressed into squares or rectangles, and then deep-fried. Additional seasoning and ingredients such as beans, zha cai, and sesame seeds may be added into the rice for added flavour. It has a similar appearance and external texture to hash browns.

Cifantuan (糍饭团) is another breakfast food consisting of a piece of youtiao tightly wrapped in cooked glutinous rice, with or without additional seasoning ingredients. Japanese onigiri resembles this Chinese food. Nuomiji is a dim sum dish consisting of glutinous rice with chicken in a lotus-leaf wrap, which is then steamed. It is served as a dim sum dish in Hong Kong, Singapore and Malaysia. Babaofan (八宝饭), or "eight treasure rice", is a dessert made from glutinous rice, steamed and mixed with lard, sugar, and eight kinds of fruits or nuts.

Hybrid Rice

Hybrid rice is grown from hybrid rice seed which is produced by growing an inbred rice variety having sterile pollen which is cross pollinated with normal pollen from adjacent rice plants of a different inbred variety. Hybrid rice therefore has two genetically different parents. As with other types of hybrids, hybrid rice typically displays heterosis (or hybrid vigor) such that when it is grown under the same conditions as comparable high-yielding inbred rice varieties it can produce up to 30% more rice. High-yield crops, like hybrid rice, are one of the most important tools for combating world food crises.

The first hybrid rice varieties were released in China. In crop breeding, although the use of heterosis in first-generation seeds is well known, its application in rice was limited because of the self-pollination character of that crop. In 1974, Chinese scientists successfully transferred the male sterility gene from wild rice to create the cytoplasmic genetic male-sterile (CMS) line and hybrid combination. The first generation of hybrid rice varieties were three-line hybrids and produced yields that were about 15%~20% greater than those of improved or high-yielding varieties of the same growth duration.

Chinese scientist Yuan Longping (the Father of Hybrid rice) is one of the most famous researchers on hybrid rice. In the 1960s, he made his seminal discovery of the genetic basis of heterosis in rice. This was a unique discovery because it had been previously thought that heterosis was not possible for self-pollinating crops such as rice. According to the *China Daily*, in 2011, Yuan developed a new hybrid rice that can produce 13.9 tons of rice per hectare.

Another Chinese agronomist, Li Zhengyou, developed the Dian (or Yunnan)-type hybrid rice, and was a pioneer in the research of high-altitude hybrid rice. He published the book *Dian-type Hybrid Rice*. Among Dian-type hybrid rices in Yunnan Province, Yuza 29 is a japonica type hybrid combination which was bred by the Rice Research Institute of Yunnan Agricultural University in 1991. At present, Yuza 29 was recognized as a good hybrid combination with respect to its characteristics of super high-yielding, rice blast resistance, and wide ecological adaptability. There was significant difference in parental heredity in Yuza 29, in which the male parent namely Nan 29 consists of the heredity of both indica and japonica rice. In 1994, Yuza 29 created a new world record of japonica rice grain yield 16.6 t/hm^2 in Binchuan, Yunnan. Up to now, Yuza 29 has covered an accumulative area of 1000 hectares in Yunnan, it will be extended as a predominant hybrid combination in the large japonica rice area of Yunnan and the Southwestern China during the next five years. This paper presented the study results on breeding procedures, integrated technologies of multiplication, seed production, and super high-yielding cultivation of Yuza 29. The study and development history of Dian-type japonica hybrid rice in Yunnan (China) had more than 30 years. The hybrid rice variety development in the project contributed significantly to increase food production in Yunnan. However, the knowledge about the performance of Dian-type hybrid rice in drought condition was lacking. A study was conducted to evaluate the characteristics of Dian-type hybrid rice in drought condition and determine the correlation between economic yield, growth rateand several agronomic traits. The results were expected to serve as basis for future proposal on cultivation of Dian-type hybrid rice in less water conditions and selection of new hybrid rice cultivars with drought tolerance. There were genetic differences in these hybrids. Of these, Dianza 35 had higher yield than the other four tested hybrids, which was suitable for planting in less water conditions. The correlation analysis showed that plot yield was highly correlated with number of filled seed setting per panicle, growth rate at 63 days after transplanting and percentage seed set, recording correlation coefficient of 0.96 and 0.93 and 0.9, respectively. The number of filled seeds per panicle, percentage seed set and growth rate during meiosis stage would be an appropriate indicators for selection of high-yielding hybrid rice with drought tolerance in a future breeding programme.

In China, hybrid rice is estimated to be planted on more than 50% of rice-growing land there and it is credited with helping the country increase its rice yields, which are among the highest within Asia. Hybrid rice is also grown in many other important rice producing countries including Indonesia, Vietnam, Myanmar, Bangladesh, India, Sri Lanka, Brazil, USA, and the Philippines. A 2010 study published by the International Rice Research Institute (IRRI), reports that the profitability of hybrid rice in three Indian states varied from being equally profitable as other rice to 34% more profitable.

Outside of China other institutes are also researching hybrid rice, including the International Rice Research Institute, which also coordinates the Hybrid Rice Development.

Wild Rice

Wild rice (Ojibwe: Manoomin, also called Canada rice, Indian rice, and water oats) are four species of grasses forming the genus *Zizania*, and the grain that can be harvested from them. The grain was historically gathered and eaten in both North America and China. While now a delicacy in North America, the grain is eaten less in China, where the plant's stem is used as a vegetable.

Wild rice is not directly related to Asian rice (*Oryza sativa*), whose wild progenitors are *O. rufipogon* and *O. nivara*, although they are close cousins, sharing the tribe Oryzeae. Wild-rice grains have a chewy outer sheath with a tender inner grain that has a slightly vegetal taste.

The plants grow in shallow water in small lakes and slow-flowing streams, often, only the flowering head of wild rice rises above the water. The grain is eaten by dabbling ducks and other aquatic wildlife, as well as by humans.

Manchurian wild rice (菰, gu), gathered from the wild, was once an important grain in ancient China. It is now very rare in the wild, and its use as a grain has completely disappeared in China, though it continues to be cultivated for its stems.

The swollen crisp white stems of Manchurian wild rice are grown as a vegetable, popular in East and Southeast Asia. The swelling occurs because of infection with the smut fungus *Ustilago esculenta*. The fungus prevents the plant from flowering, so the crop is propagated asexually, the infection being passed from mother plant to daughter plant. Harvest must be made between about 120 days and 170 days after planting, after the stem begins to swell but before the infection reaches its reproductive stage, when the stem will begin to turn black and eventually disintegrate into fungal spores.

The vegetable is especially common in China, where it is known as gaosun (高笋) or jiaobai (茭白). Other names which may be used in English include water rice and water bamboo.

Cooked wild rice

Nutrition and safety

Typically sold as a dried whole grain, wild rice is high in protein, the amino acid lysine and dietary fiber, and low in fat. Nutritional analysis shows wild rice to be second only to oats in protein content per 100 calories. Like true rice, it does not contain gluten. It is also a good source of certain minerals and B vitamins. One cup of cooked wild rice provides 5% or more of the daily value of thiamin, riboflavin, iron, and potassium; 10% or more of the daily value of niacin, b6, folate, magnesium, phosphorus; 15% of zinc; and over 20% of manganese.

Wild rice seeds can be infected by the highly toxic fungus ergot, which is dangerous if eaten. Infected grains have pink or purplish blotches or growths of the fungus, from the size of a seed to several times larger.

Words & Expressions

glutinous /'gluːtənəs/ *adj.* 黏的，胶质的
negligible /'neglɪdʒəbl/ *adj.* 微不足道的，不值一提的
gluten /'gluːtən/ *n.* 面筋，麸质，谷蛋白
translucent /trænz'luːsnt/ *adj.* 透明的，半透明的
hybrid /'haɪbrɪd/ *adj.* 杂交的；混合的，杂种的；*n.* 混合物
cytoplasmic genetic male-sterile (CMS) 细胞质遗传雄性不育
heterosis /ˌhetə'rəʊsɪs/ *n.* [遗] 杂种优势
panicle /'pænɪk(ə)l/ *n.* 圆锥花序
stem /stem/ *n.* （植物、灌木的）茎，干；*v.* 去梗，去柄，阻止，遏制，起源于
niacin /'naɪəsɪn/ *n.* [生化] 烟酸，尼克酸
folate /'fəʊleɪt/ *n.* 叶酸
Dian-type Hybrid Rice 滇型杂交水稻

Notes

Glutinous rice (*Oryza sativa* var. *glutinosa*; also called sticky rice, sweet rice or waxy rice) is a type of rice grown mainly in Southeast and East Asia and the eastern parts of South Asia, which has opaque grains, very low amylose content, and is especially sticky when cooked.

糯米（禾本科稻属，又称糯米、甜米或蜡米）是一种主要生长在东南亚、东亚和南亚东部的水稻，颗粒不透明，直链淀粉含量很低，煮熟时特别黏稠。

Reading Comprehension

Ⅰ. **Each piece of the following information is given in one of the paragraphs in the passage. Identify the paragraph from which the information is derived and put the corresponding number in the space provided.**

(　　) 1. Glutinous rice has been cultivated for at least two thousand years in China.

(　　) 2. Glutinous rice, also called sticky rice, is a type of rice grown mainly in Southeast and East Asia and the eastern parts of South Asia.

(　　) 3. The improved rice varieties, in terms of yield, adopted throughout Asia were non-glutinous。

(　　) 4. The color of milled glutinous rice is white.

(　　) 5. Glutinous rice is distinguished from other types of rice in the amount of amylose, and amylopectin.

(　　) 6. Glutinous rice is always ground to make glutinous rice flour for niangao and tangyuan.

II. Decide whether the statements are true (T) or false (F) according to the passage.

(   ) 1. Glutinous rice or glutinous rice flour are used in many Chinese varieties of dim sum.

(   ) 2. Unmilled glutinous may present brown or black color.

(   ) 3. The difference of glutinous rice from other types has been traced to a single mutation that was selected for by farmers.

(   ) 4. The rice has been recorded in the region for at least 2100 years.

(   ) 5. Steamed bun is especially eaten during the Dragon Boat Festival.

III. Discuss the following questions.

1. What are the features of glutinous rice?
2. What colors do varieties of glutinous rice have?

Text C 稻文化 / Rice Culture

Cultural Roles of Rice in China

Chinese culture, boasting a lengthy history, is composed of numerous sub-cultures. The agricultural way of life, centered around rice, has played an important part in the country's history.

For thousands of years, the Chinese have been diligently cultivating their land. Blood, sweat and tears have been shed over their soil in the pursuit of favorable harvests. This reliance on the land for so many thousands of years accounts for China's strong rural essence. The need for rice production has led the Chinese to pay particular attention to irrigation technologies, improving cultivation. The agricultural way of life, centered around rice, has had a strong influence on the social, economic, political and ideological developments of ancient China. In this sense, traditional Chinese culture may be considered a "rice culture".

While exploring the status of rice in Chinese culture a number of developments become apparent. According to Professor Zhang Deci, an expert on cultivation, rice first grew when people, who had lived mainly on hunting, fishing, and fruit collecting, happened to leave some seeds in low-lying areas. Later, these people began developing the land, making it more suitable for farming. Weeding, rice transplanting, and irrigating all originated in the Yellow River Valley region in the north, and Hanshui Basin region in the northwest. To date, traces of rice have been found in Hemudu of Yuyao, Zhejiang Province,

Yangshao of Mianchi, Henan Province, Dachendun of Feidong, Anhui Province, Miaoshan of Nanjing and Xianlidun of Wuxi in Jiangsu Province, Qianshanyang of Wuxing, Zhejiang Province, Qujialing and Zhujiazui of Jingshan, Shijiahe of Tianmen, and Fangyingtai of Wuchang in Hubei Province. Archaeologists have confirmed that China started planting rice at least 3000 to 4000 years ago. In the 1970s, seeds of long-grained non-glutinous rice were unearthed from the Neolithic ruins at Hemudu in Yuyao, Zhejiang Province, the earliest records of rice planting in China, and the world.

By the time the western Zhou Dynasty was in power, rice had become well accepted and extremely important, as can be seen from inscriptions on bronze vessels used as containers for storing rice. At this time, rice was a central part of aristocratic banquets. During the Spring and Autumn period, rice became an important part of the diets for Chinese people. Later, in Southern China, especially with the development of meticulously intensive farming techniques during the Han Dynasty, rice rose to occupy an important position in Chinese culture.

The cultivation of rice led to the development of an economic lifecycle centered around agriculture: ploughing in spring, weeding in summer, harvesting in autumn, and hoarding in winter. In ancient China, vast amounts of land, including the present middle and lower reaches of the Yangtze River region and North China region, were suitable for planting rice, with most Chinese working the land in particular ways during the different seasons.

Rice farming influenced many other aspects of the old Chinese economy. For instance, to be viable Chinese farming depended on sophisticated irrigation techniques. The importance of irrigation was outlined in the *Twenty-Four Histories*, a collection of books chronicling 4000 years of Chinese history, which recorded dynastic histories from distant antiquity up until the Ming Dynasty. Books discussing rice agriculture appeared as early as the Warring States Period, demonstrating the long history of China's agronomy. *Daopin (Strains of Rice)*, by Huang Xingsi, a book specializing in the rice planting techniques of the Ming Dynasty, was widely regarded as a complete collection detailing the improvements of rice through its many strains. The book also illustrates the significance of rice agriculture in traditional Chinese economy.

China was built on agriculture. During the period before the Qin Dynasty, rice had become a specially prepared food. It was also used to brew wines and offered as a sacrifice to the Gods. What's more, rice was delicately made into different kinds of food, which played an important role in a number of traditional Chinese festivities.

Firstly, rice is a central part of the Spring Festival (or lunar New Year) Eve dinner. On this occasion, Chinese families make New Year's cake and steamed sponge cake from flour turned from glutinous rice. The cake is called "gao" in Chinese, a homophony to another "gao," meaning high. People eat these cakes in the hope of a better harvest and higher status in the New Year. The cakes and the New Year's dinner symbolize people's wishes for a better future.

Secondly, rice dumplings are made on the 15th night of the 1st lunar month. This is the first day the full moon can be seen each New Year. People eat rice dumplings, known as yuanxiao in the north and tangyuan in the south (yuan means of satisfaction in Chinese), hoping everything will turn out as they wish.

Thirdly, zongzi, eaten during the Dragon Boat Festival on the 5th day of the 5th lunar month, is also made of glutinous rice. It is said that people eat zongzi on this day to remember Qu Yuan, an official of Chu State (about 340 BC—278 BC), who committed suicide by jumping into the Miluo River. People throw zongi into the river to prevent fish eating Qu Yuan's body.

Fourthly, rice is made into "double nine" festival cakes on the 9th day of the 9th lunar month each year. As people have just harvested their crops during autumn they can make these cakes with fresh new rice. Many people also follow the tradition of climbing a mountain on this day.

Finally, people eat porridge on the 8th day of the 12th lunar month. The porridge is made with rice, cereals, beans, nuts and dried fruit. It is said that Sakyamuni attained Buddhahood on this day, drinking chyle presented to him by a shepherdess, which he believes led him to enlightenment. As a result people bathe Buddha statues and eat porridge on this day.

Ancient traditions surround growing and storage of essential food grain. Before Hinduism, Buddhism, and Christianity, the predominant religions in Southeast Asia, especially China, revolved around rice, ecology, and the environment. Throughout Asia, rice is still considered sacred and the ritual of harvesting rice has shaped Southeast Asian cultures and tradition for centuries.

Throughout history, this grain has meant more than just sustenance, in many cultures it is a central element in both culinary and spiritual practices. Today, more than half the world's population is sustained by it, and in many parts of Asia, a meal is not considered a meal unless rice is served. Celebrations are often linked to its harvest and planting, such as the Pongal Festival in Southern India, where Hindus, in honor of the new harvest, cook rice in pots until it boils over. Rice worship also takes place each day in places like Tibet, where Buddhists offer a bowl of white rice as a daily offering. And in Indonesia, the rice goddess, Dewi Sri, is much revered, as is rice, which is believed to have a spirit or soul.

Rice has informed many aspects of Southeast Asian village tradition, including religion and social order. In many parts of China, a three-class system has ordered society hierarchically. Those who owned land for cultivating rice were the most powerful. Rank was noted in the size and quantity of the rice. The size of a person's house and rice granaries distinguished the wealthy from the poor. In many places, rice granaries have been designed to resemble human houses, indicating the close connection between humans and their rice.

A great deal of time and detail is dedicated to creating elaborate storage facilities and containers for rice. Special ceremonies may take place when rice is brought in from the fields and installed into the granary. All the areas where rice is found, such as fields, granaries, and distilleries, are considered sacred spaces.

For the Toraja peoples in South Sulawesi, Indonesia, rice rituals are often carried out in the morning and rice is often related to rising suns. Many of the Toraja granaries are decorated with bright gold sunburst designs. The sun is often depicted as "the crowning element" of the granary. Granaries are art spaces for the people. Some of the artisans are fed and paid for their full time work.

In Asian cultures, rice is strongly "associated with women and fertility" and religious ceremonies have been conducted mainly for "assurance of rice, fecundity of domestic animals, and propagation of human species". Throughout Southeast Asia and specifically in Indonesia, "people harvest rice with small finger knives so the rice goddess doesn't become upset". Both in Indonesia and the Philippines, senior skilled women have traditionally used delicate hand knives to carefully select the seed rice for future harvests. Many Southeast Asian cultures believe in a female rice deity and still today they make offerings and practice rituals to honor her.

The rice mother

In Java and Bali, the rice goddess is known as Dewi Sri. Among the Tai Yong of Northern Thailand, she is called Mae Ku'sok, and to other Southeast Asian cultures she is simply referred to as the "Rice Mother" or "Rice Maiden".

The Tai are the single largest ethnolinguistic group across mainland Southeast Asia. The Tai believe that the Rice Mother inhabits the rice field, protecting the harvest and nurturing the seed rice. The Rice Mother loves textiles and jewelry. The villagers plant seeds next to the marker and use those seedlings for the next year.

In some rituals, a symbolic body of the Rice Mother is made out of straw and serves as the marker, which is then tied to a straw latticework and attached to a vertical bamboo stick so that the marker can stand upright in a special corner of the rice field. Offerings of meat, betel nut, white homespun cotton cloth, silver jewelry, and sarongs are placed next to the marker by a priest.

Southeast Asian rice rituals are as varied as they are numerous. Every twelve years the ceremony takes place to celebrate "good harvest". Carried out in sacred fields, the grounds are marked by three special types of trees: sandalwood, banyan, and lamba. The ceremony usually takes place in October or November. Families sacrifice small female pigs and offer the collarbone of the pig, which is a symbol of fecundity. The ceremony begins "in the dead of night". They will illuminate the sacred ground with huge bonfires of hardwood that has been dried and seasoned for months. The Toraja have so far been able to maintain their indigenous religious belief system and rituals despite the fact that they are a minority ethnic group, living on a majority-Muslim island.

Technologies erode old traditions

Many of these rituals and the religions themselves are endangered. With modernization and new technologies rapidly spreading throughout Southeast Asian villages, the way rice is cultivated and harvested is changing as individuals and corporations try "to develop faster-producing grain". For more than two decades, the International Rice Research Institute, headquartered in the Philippines, has been introducing a small number of varieties that have gradually replaced a much larger number of highly diverse varieties that have been used for centuries. This has had devastating effects on the rice traditions and cultures of Southeast Asian villages. Rice is now frequently grown as a commercial product rather than through subsistence farming. With the use of new rice varieties, pesticides, fertilizers, and new technologies for harvesting rice, the rice culture and the delicate ecosystems that rice supports are changing dramatically.

The traditional rice field is full of life. Even after rice is harvested, there are eels, frogs, and small fish that people gather. Year after year, decade after decade, and millennia after millennia the rice field is renewed". But now all this may come to a halt.

The abundance of life that is supported by a traditional rice field ecosystem in rice terraces three thousand feet above sea level. During the rainy season, fish are harvested in these terraces. Ducks come after the rice harvest to eat the gleanings and lay eggs. Life is born and re-born, there's a constant cycle of birth and rebirth with rice. If measures are not taken to preserve this rich history and tradition. It is sadly predicted that an unfortunate decline in rice culture and its associated art.

The Myth and Legend of the Origin of Rice

Although they have different histories, cultures and societies, all the countries of east and southeast Asia have rice as a common denominator. It is not simply that these peoples cultivate rice, they all have customs, rituals and myths concerning rice which serve as threads to bind them together. Rice culture is extremely important as the common inheritance of these regions.

Myths concerning the origin of rice take many forms. Some have points in common with myths related to other crops. One of these, which is widely current in such parts of the region as Indonesia and Malaysia, tells how crops originated from the corpse of a murdered god or human being. Myths of this kind often relate that other crops originated at the same time as rice. In Java, according to some versions, fruit bearing plants originated from the corpse of a young girl; dry land rice from the navel; coconut palms from the head and genitals; ripened fruit dangled from both hands, and fruit originated from the legs and ripened in the ground. Among the Manggarai people of Flores Island, it is said that rice and maize originated from the corpse of a murdered child. According to the Japanese classic Kojiki (Record of ancient matters), compiled in 712 AD, Susanoo slew the food goddess Ohogetsu-hime. Silkworms came from her head, rice seeds from both eyes, millet from both ears, red beans from her nose, wheat from her genitals, and soybeans from her buttocks.

Many mountain peoples of the southeast Asian mainland and islands sacrifice domestic animals such as water buffalo and pigs as an agricultural ritual. Some plain dwelling peoples of the region, such as the Lao of Laos, also sacrifice water buffalo. The motives underlying this practice are varied. It is believed that the flesh of the animal is presented to the gods in exchange for the gods' gift of an abundant rice harvest. It is also thought that magical power (mana) contained in animal blood promotes the growth of plants.

Given the view that death is a premise of life, animal sacrifice has points in common with myths that relate the origin of crops from corpses. In the southeast Asian islands, myth and sacrifice frequently accompany one another. Yet, on the mainland, despite the fact that animal sacrifice is widespread, myths which relate the origin of rice from corpses hardly appear at all.

Another important form of rice cultivation myth refers to the stealing of crop seeds. These myths are found not only in east and southeast Asia but are also widespread among the agricultural peoples of Africa and the Americas. Furthermore, these myths are not exclusively tied to rice cultivation but are also applied to the cultivation of sorghum in Africa and to maize in America. In Samoa, taro origin myths also take this form. In parts of East Asia, amongst the mountain people of Taiwan, for example, this stealing motif is found in myths concerning the origins of millet.

It is said that the ancestors of the Miao people of Sichuan, China, did not have the necessary seed to sow their fields. They set free a green bird which then flew up to the rice granary of the heaven god and returned with the heavenly rice seed and tare. A myth of the Minahassa region of Sulawesi (Indonesia) recounts how a man went up to heaven and returned to earth with unhulled rice concealed in a wound in his leg.

A conspicuous feature of the rice cultivation rituals of east and southeast Asia is the frequent appearance of the concept of a rice soul. The Lamet, slash-and-burn rice cultivators of Laos, constitute a representative example of ancient rice cultivation rituals which are accompanied by this idea. They perform rituals which include strict taboos at each point in the cultivation process, and their concept of the rice soul is similar to those of many of the peoples inhabiting the islands of Southeast Asia.

Rice is an integral part of many cultures folklore. In Myanmar, the Kachins were sent forth from the center of the Earth with rice seeds and were directed to a country where life would be perfect and rice would grow well. In Bali, Lord Vishnu caused the Earth to give birth to rice and the God Indra taught people how to raise it. And in China rice is the gift of animals. Legend says after a disastrous flooding all plants had been destroyed and no food was available. One day a dog ran through the fields to the people with rice seeds hanging from his tail. The people planted the seeds, rice grew and hunger disappeared. All of these stories and many others have rice as their foundation and for generations people have believed these lores of Rice. A study of Han Chinese communities found that a history of farming rice makes cultures more psychologically interdependent, whereas a history of farming wheat makes cultures more independent.

Rice plays an important role in certain religions and popular beliefs. In many cultures relatives will scatter rice during or towards the end of a wedding ceremony in front of the bride and groom. The pounded rice ritual is conducted during weddings in Nepal. The bride gives a leaf plate full of pounded rice to the groom after he requests it politely from her. In the Philippines rice wine, popularly known as tapuy, is used for important occasions such as weddings, rice harvesting ceremonies and other celebrations.

Dewi Sri is the traditional rice goddess of the Javanese, Sundanese, and Balinese people in Indonesia. Most rituals involving Dewi Sri are associated with the mythical origin attributed to the rice plant, the staple food of the region. In Thailand, a similar rice deity is known as Phosop, she is a deity more related to ancient local folklore than a goddess of a structured, mainstream religion. The same female rice deity is known as Po Ino Nogar in Cambodia and as Nang Khosop in Laos. Ritual offerings are made during the different stages of rice production to propitiate the Rice Goddess in the corresponding culture.

Regarding the dream about the rice, its meaning may be the symbol of nourishment, health and life. Dreams related to rice might indicate well-being. Symbolism could be shown that rice is a food that helps to live and survive. Thus, the dreams related to rice might depict one's well-being, health and prosperity.

Words & Expressions

inscription /ɪnˈskrɪpʃn/ n. 题词，铭文，刻印
vessel /ˈvesl/ n.（人或动物的）血管，（植物的）导管，船，舰，（盛液体用的）容器
aristocratic /ˌærɪstəˈkrætɪk/ adj. 贵族的，有贵族特征的
granary /ˈɡrænəri/ n. 谷仓，粮仓，盛产粮食的地区
collarbone /ˈkɒləbəʊn/ n. 锁骨
composed of 由…组成

Reading Comprehension

I. Each piece of the following information is given in one of the paragraphs in the passage. Identify the paragraph from which the information is derived and put the corresponding number in the space provided.

(　　) 1. During the Spring and Autumn period, rice became a vital part of the diets for Chinese.

(　　) 2. Chinese farming depended on sophisticated irrigation techniques to be viable.

(　　) 3. Chinese have been pursuing the harvest over the land for thousands of years, which is considered as the essence of rural reliance.

(　　) 4. Chinese agricultural culture is centered around rice.

(　　) 5. Based on an expert on cultivation, rice first grew when people, who had lived mainly on hunting, fishing, and fruit collecting, happened to leave some seeds in low-lying areas.

(　　) 6. Rice led to the development of an economic life cycle centered around agriculture.

II. **Decide whether the statements are true (T) or false (F) according to the passage.**

(　　) 1. Rice agriculture appeared as early as the Warring States Period, demonstrating the long history of China's agronomy, indicated by the official agency.

(　　) 2. China was built on agriculture.

(　　) 3. Rice is a central part of the Spring Festival Eve dinner.

(　　) 4. Baozi, eaten during the Dragon Boat Festival on the 5th day of the 5th lunar month, is also made of glutinous rice.

(　　) 5. By the time the western Zhou Dynasty was in power, rice had become well accepted and extremely important.

III. **Discuss the following questions.**

1. What are the characteristics of Chinese rice culture?

2. What kinds of food made of rice played an important role in traditional Chinese festivities?

参考文献
Reference

胡宗锋, 2000. 中国传统文化习俗 [M]. 西安: 西安地图出版社.

胡宗锋, 罗宾·吉尔班克, 2015. 中国传统文化习俗 [M]. 西安: 西安电子科技大学出版社.

李逸安, 高巍, 刘士聪, 2006. 节日习俗: 中国传统文化双语读本 [M]. 北京: 人民文学出版社.

张桃林, 2014. 农谚 800 句 [M]. 北京: 中国农业出版社.

彭建波, 等, 2017. 皮影数字博物馆 [EB/OL]. (2017-11-22) [2022-04-23]. http://shadow.caa.edu.cn.

吴圣正, 2019. 中国传统文化概说 [M]. 北京: 人民出版社.

Zhang T L, 2017. A Selected Collection of Chinese Agricultural Proverbs [M]. Beijing: China Agriculture Press.

Pang K, 2021. The 24 Solar Terms [EB/OL]. (2021-12-31) [2022-04-23]. https://www.chinahighlights.com/ festivals/the-24-solar-terms.htm.

REBECA TOLEDO, 2008. How to celebrate Chinese farmers Harvest Festival [EB/OL]. (2008-7-19) [2022-4-23]. http://www.bjreview.com/Lifestyle/201807/ t20180720_800135872.html.

ZHAO YIMENG, 2019. Farmers to hold major events along Yangtze to celebrate harvest [EB/OL]. (2019-09-01) [2022-04-23]. http://www.chinadaily.com.cn/a/202109/01/WS612f261ea310efa1bd66ca12. html.

GUO XTAO HONG, 2021. Farmers' harvest festival marked in Yanqing [EB/OL]. (2021-9-23) [2022-4-23]. http://www.china.org.cn/ travel/2021-09/23/content_777 70571.htm.

HUANG X., KURATA N, WEI X, et al, 2012. A map of rice genome variation reveals the origin of cultivated rice [J]. Nature (490): 497-501.

BARBER E J W, 1992. Prehistoric textiles: the development of cloth in the Neolithic and Bronze Ages with special reference to the Aegean (reprint, illustrated ed.)[M]. New Jersey: Princeton University Press.

GOOD I L, KENOYER J M, MEADOW R H, 2009. New Evidence for Early Silk in the Indus Civilization[J]. Archaeometry, 51 (3): 457-466.

VAINKER S 2004. Chinese silk: A cultural history[M]. New Jersey: Rutgers University Press.

BISCH-KNADEN S, et al, 2014. Anatomical and functional analysis of domestication effects on the olfactory system of the silkmoth Bombyx mori[J]. Proceedings of the Royal Society of London B: Biological Sciences, 281 (1774): 20132582.

TANAKA K, et al, 2009. Highly selective tuning of a silkworm olfactory receptor to a key mulberry leaf volatile[J]. Current Biology, 19 (11): 881-890.

TANG R, et al, 2016. Electrophysiological responses and reproductive behavior of fall webworm moths (Hyphantria cunea drury) are influenced by volatile compounds from its mulberry host (*Morus alba* L.)[J]. Insects, 7 (2): 19.

LIU X, et al, 2004. Quantification and purification of mulberry anthocyanins with macroporous resins[J]. Journal of Biomedicine & Biotechnology (5): 326-331.

MAIR V H, HOH E, 2009. The true history of tea[M]. London: Thames & Hudson.

LU H, et al, 2016. Earliest tea as evidence for one branch of the Silk Road across the Tibetan Plateau[J]. Nature (6): 18955.

SIMMONS M, 2009. The Amazing World of Rice: with 150 Recipes for Pilafs, Paellas, Puddings, and More[M]. New York: Harper Collins e-books.

ALFORD J, DUGUID N, 2003. Seductions of Rice[M]. Hoboken: Artisan.

WILLY H, et al, 2010. "Growth and Production of Rice". Soils, Plant Growth and Crop Production Volume II [M]. Oxford: EOLSS Publishers.

NORMILE D, 1997. Yangtze seen as earliest rice site[J]. Science, 275 (5298): 309-310.

DA V, LU B, TOMOOK N, 2008. The evolving story of rice evolution[J]. Plant Science, 174 (4): 394-408.

SIGLEY G, 2015. Tea and China's rise: tea, nationalism and culture in the 21st century[J]. International Communication of Chinese Culture, 2 (3): 319-341.

HINSCH B, 2016. The Rise of tea culture in China: the invention of the individual[M]. London: Cambridge.

LI X, 1993. Chinese Tea Culture[J]. The Journal of Popular Culture, 27 (2): 75-90.